# Opposites
# Attract

## TIM LAHAYE

Distributed By
Choice Books of Gulf States
6115 Old Pascagoula Rd.
Theodore, AL 36582
Your Response Appreciated

**HARVEST HOUSE PUBLISHERS**
Eugene, Oregon 97402

Except where otherwise indicated, all Scripture quotations in this book are taken from the New King James Version, Copyright © 1979, 1980, 1982 by Thomas Nelson, Inc., Publishers. Used by permission.

Verses marked NASB are taken from the New American Standard Bible, © 1960, 1962, 1963, 1968, 1971, 1972, 1973, 1975, 1977 by The Lockman Foundation. Used by permission.

Verses marked NIV are taken from the Holy Bible, New International Version ®, Copyright © 1973, 1978, 1984 by the International Bible Society. Used by permission of Zondervan Publishing House. The "NIV" and "New International Version" trademarks are registered in the United States Patent and Trademark Office by International Bible Society.

*Cover by Terry Dugan Design, Minneapolis, Minnesota*

The section "The 12 Blends" in chapter 8 was adapted from Tim LaHaye's *Understanding the Male Temperament* (Grand Rapids: Fleming H. Revell, a division of Baker Book House, 1977, 1996), chapter 6. Used by permission.

Published in association with the literary agency of Alive Communications, Colorado Springs, Colorado.

## OPPOSITES ATTRACT

Copyright © 1991 by Tim LaHaye
Published by Harvest House Publishers
Eugene, Oregon 97402

Library of Congress Cataloging-in-Publication Data

LaHaye, Tim F.
    Opposites attract / Tim LaHaye.
        p.  cm.
    Rev. ed. of: I love you, buy why are we so different? 1991.
    ISBN 1-56507-952-3
        1. Marriage—Religious aspects—Christianity.    2. Typology
(Psychology)   3. Temperament.   I. LaHaye, Tim F.   I love you,
but why are we so different?   II. Title.
BV835.L27    1998
248.8'44—dc21                                              98-5767
                                                                  CIP

**Printed in the United States of America.**

98  99  00  01  02  03  04  /  BP  /  10  9  8  7  6  5  4  3  2  1

To Dr. Henry Brandt,

one of the first Christian psychologists
to scrutinize the theories of psychology
and hold them accountable to the Word of
God. He not only introduced me to the
Spirit-filled life, which helped to enrich
the relationship between my wife Beverly
and me, but he taught me to use biblical
principles in counseling people. He is
easily one of the three most significant
influences in both of our lives. But we are
not unique. He has helped thousands of
Christian workers in both this country and
abroad.

# Contents

# Two Ways to Do It

If there are two ways to do anything, my wife will surely choose one way as naturally as I choose the other.

My wife likes to get to the airport one hour before liftoff; with me only two minutes count when I catch a plane—one minute before and one minute after!

My wife almost never exceeds the speed limit; if I don't watch it, I edge 4-1/2 miles above the limit—just slow enough to avoid getting a ticket yet fast enough not to waste time.

My wife thinks the gas tank is empty as soon as the gauge registers half-full. I have been known to run on fumes!

My wife buys only two or three of anything when she goes to the grocery store; I buy enough for a month.

My wife compulsively balances the checkbook to the penny; I have been known to accept the bank's stated balance as long as it's "close" to mine (how can anyone challenge a computer?).

My wife is an introvert who rarely offers her opinion unless asked; I'm an extrovert who regularly volunteers his opinion, whether anyone wants it or not.

My wife is an early riser but often takes a nap in the evening; I'm a nocturnal person who does his best work at night—but wakes up in the morning like death warmed over.

My wife likes to plan everything she does in advance; I prefer to make snap decisions—which are frequently wrong.

My wife is an impeccable speller; I thank God every day for dictionaries and computer "spell-check" programs.

My wife wears only well-coordinated outfits; I do too—but she picks them out for me!

As founder and president of Concerned Women for America, the largest women's organization in America, my wife loves personnel and administration; I'm an entrepreneur who has launched 14 different Christian organizations and turned all but one of them over to other people to run. Preferring not to manage people, I would rather inspire and motivate, then set them free to serve the Lord.

My wife, who never raises her voice, is so nice that she makes people feel sorry for her when she has to fire them; I have spent much of my life apologizing and bandaging up wounded psyches and injured spirits. Maybe that explains why her one organization is larger than all 14 of mine put together.

My wife is a lover of music and the fine arts; I am a sports nut who seldom troubles himself over the survival of "culture," particularly if I have to endure it.

My wife is a slow and particular eater; I consume anything—too fast and too much.

When we married, Bev was a gracious but fearful young woman; I was forceful and filled with anger. (Thank God for the ministry of the Holy Spirit!)

My wife and I are about as opposite as two people can be—yet with God's help we have experienced an ideal marriage. It was not always that way, for we faced major adjustments, beginning the first day after our two-day honeymoon. Although our temperaments represent ends of the spectrum, today we are each other's best friend and favorite person.

Our only regret is that we never heard of the temperament theory when we were married, so obviously we didn't know why opposites attract each other in marriage or how to adjust to each other. But thanks to Nia Jones, who originally challenged me to write this book, and to Bob Hawkins at Harvest House Publishers, for pressing me to finish it, you can save yourself years of frustration and so-called "personality clashes" by reading this book.

With God's help and your cooperation, any two people, regardless of their contrasting temperaments, background, and training, can adjust to their opposite partner and build a beautiful, fulfilling relationship for a lifetime.

This book is not intended to be read, enjoyed, and forgotten. It will hopefully change your life and marriage, if that is your need, or enable you to help others who would benefit from its precepts. Unless they have discovered the principles for marital happiness revealed in this book, everyone you know needs them. Read on—you won't be disappointed, I promise!

— *Tim LaHaye*

# PART ONE

# *Why Opposites Attract*

# 1

# Help!
# I Married a Sanguine!

No two people can enjoy a more emotionally sur-charged honeymoon better than Sparky Sanguine and Martha Melancholy. Both possess the richest emotions of the four basic temperaments.

Sparky is the fun-loving superextrovert with personality, charisma, and charm to burn. He is the life of the party who invariably responds warmly to people. To him, as Shake-speare observed, "All the world's a stage."

He is an enthusiastic, feeling-oriented person who can easily be moved to tears by the sad moods of his friends, or to joy and laughter by the happiness of others. Friendliness personified, he can and usually does make friends out of total strangers in a matter of seconds. He loves to please others—and oh, does he enjoy their praise! Sanguines never proceed through life unnoticed.

Martha Melancholy, on the other hand, is usually a somber introvert who wears her feelings on her sleeves. As a rule she will have a better-than-average IQ, possess strong analytical powers, and be a perfectionist. No one has a better appreciation for music, art, and theater than someone with Martha's temperament. She does not make friends easily but is extremely loyal to the few friends she has. She is a master at color coordination and is perfection personified—a chic dresser with hardly a hair out of place, makeup always coordinated with her outfit. Her natural inhibitions and fear of making a mistake often keep her from sharing in public her thoughts and talents. Harboring deep feelings and concern for other people, she is happiest when sacrificing for the good of others.

For some reason, a woman of Martha's temperament lacks self-confidence even though she is usually highly gifted. Unless moved emotionally, she says very little in public, and when she does, for days afterward she relives every word and condemns herself for imagined mistakes. But that is how she and Sparky got together.

Martha attended a party for about 20 people at a friend's home. However, the evening was a bummer, primarily because no Sanguines were present. Actually, the hostess had made the mistake of inviting only one Sanguine, which is a social blunder: You can't have a good party without at least one Sanguine, so always invite three. One will forget to come, another will lose the directions, and the third will be late.

Just about the time Martha had decided the party was heading downhill, the doorbell rang and the host opened the door. There he was, Sparky Sanguine!

You will never believe what Sparky was thinking just before he pushed the doorbell button. "Sparky, tonight why don't you keep your big mouth shut? Give other people a chance to say something. You don't always have to be the life of the party." And he meant it—until the door opened and he spotted another person. And then he realized that a whole roomful of warm, vibrant people were inviting him onto their stage. That did it! As if a button in his brain was pressed, he instantly went into his act, strode onto the stage (the living room of his friend's house), and began his theatrical delivery. The life of the party had arrived. Greeting everyone as a long-lost friend, he didn't so much as apologize for being 45 minutes late. He just commenced with his round of endless jokes and humorous comments, and before they knew it the other guests began to match his mood, the party came to life, and everyone was having a good time.

About 11:30 his battery started to run down (and so did his supply of jokes), so he excused himself, slipped out to the car, and started to drive home. As he tromped down on the accelerator of his big gas-guzzling monster, he was reprimanding himself. "Sparky, you did it again! When will you ever learn to be quiet? (Never in this life!) Why can't you be like Martha?" Yes, he had observed her carefully! Not a hair out of place, beautiful to behold, and, naturally, everything coordinated—from the makeup on her eyelids to the plastic veneer of her shoes. "She's obviously an intelligent young woman," he thought. "She laughed at all my jokes!" Abruptly he added, "Why don't you call her for a date as soon as you get home?"

As Sparky plotted his next move, Martha was driving her little gas-saving minicar home from the party, thinking, "Martha, when are you ever going to break out of your shell and join the party?" She was contemplating all the clever remarks she had longed to insert into the conversation— but never did. "Why can't you be more like Sparky—free-spirited and uninhibited? What a man!"

The phone was ringing as she entered her apartment. It was Sparky! He invited her to dinner the following night, and she "just happened to have the night open." That date launched a whirlwind courtship which ended in a church wedding and their emotionally exotic honeymoon in Hawaii.

If only their honeymoon haven could have remained a permanent residence! But life in the real world does not extend the romantic bliss of honeymoons. Our scene changes to Monday morning, the first day of their return to work. Martha awakens to the off-key sounds of Sparky singing in the shower and suddenly realizes that she must now prepare his first "burnt offering," as he later described it. But as he likes to tell their friends, "That's okay. She said she worshiped me."

After inhaling his breakfast, Sparky rushes out the door to work, and Martha reaches her moment of truth. Shuffling back to the bedroom, she notices for the first time that it is in shambles. In the middle of her unmade bed lies his wet towel, and clothes from the night before are scattered all over the room, from the back of the chair to the floor. Trying to enact the role of the dutiful wife, she begins to pick up his clothes, promising herself, "I'll just have to teach him to take better care of his things." (The fact that his mother had tried it and failed doesn't register—at the time.)

As Martha opens the closet door, his clothes fall off their hooks to the floor. Suddenly she realizes that she is "married to a hook-er." You are probably aware that there are two kinds of people as judged by their closets: "hook-ers and hang-ers." Hang-ers are organized people who put everything neatly on hangers—pants in one section, then shirts, coats, and ties. Hook-ers simply pile things onto the nearest hook. Martha discovers that she has married a man who can pile nine pieces of clothing on one hook—until someone opened the closet door.

Extending her education as a young bride, she enters the bathroom, only to find it in worse condition than the bedroom. Sparky has used every towel on the racks—even the expensive decorator towel. The medicine-cabinet door is open, everything from the deodorant can to his hairspray is strewn all over the countertop, and she is startled to find beard chips in the wash bowl. But the coup de grace confronts her in the form of the toothpaste tube: He had squeezed it in the middle! When she decides to brush her teeth—only to find that her toothbrush is already wet—she collapses into a despondent heap.

Now I ask you, do you think these two lovebirds will have an adjustment problem? You better believe it! Unless they know how to accept each other and are willing to improve themselves, they will quickly destroy their relationship. Their love will turn to hate, and they will become another divorce statistic—unless they use the marriage adjustment techniques described later in this book.

But Sparky and Martha aren't alone. Other temperament combinations experience the same problems!

# 2
OPPSITES
*Attract*

# Woe Is Me—
# I Married a Choleric

Rocky Choleric and Phyllis Phlegmatic met at a Christian college. Three years older than she, he had spent two years in the Army before enrolling and had given up a football scholarship to attend that particular school in order to study for the ministry. (She had yielded her life to God to be a missionary.) They were assigned to the same dining room table for three weeks. As usual, Rocky came to the table looking for the most datable girls, and sat next to Phyllis. When he discovered that they both hailed from the same city, they strolled out of the dining room talking excitedly—and have been together ever since.

Phyllis found Rocky a fascinating person. He was obviously a strong-willed and opinionated man who knew where he was going and what he wanted to do. He questioned everything at the school, from the rules to the role models, and she had all she could do to keep him from getting expelled for griping. In fact, by the time they met (three weeks into the school year) he had stirred up so much trouble that he had garnered 149 demerits—one short of expulsion!

Above all, Phyllis favored Rocky because he was decisive. Preferring not to make decisions, she felt comfortable

19

letting him steer the course of their relationship. Because he was also dynamic and imaginative, listening to him dream about the future was most exciting. The possibility of failure never entered his head, and he was always vigorously engaged in a variety of activities. Because he was not the best student in the school, Phyllis helped him in the classes they shared—and during the second semester Rocky saw to it that they took most of the same classes. Somehow, even though it was against the school rules, he always seemed to arrange seats next to each other. Three other boys attempted to date her, but Rocky somehow managed to outmaneuver them all. Phyllis relished their relationship—no decisions to make, no wondering whom she was dating each weekend, no demands to plan their activities. Rocky always had a plan. Little did she realize that *she* was his plan!

Rocky was instantly enamored with Phyllis. She was very feminine, soft-spoken, and gentle; nothing seemed to ruffle her. His friends commended his choice of this pleasant, well-dressed, and attractive young woman who obviously liked him and followed his leadership, never questioning his decisions and always supporting his last-minute cramming for exams. Because her analytical skills enabled her to determine in advance almost every question the professor would ask, studying together not only united them but improved Rocky's grades.

Before long Rocky began to realize what a perfect minister's wife she would make—not to mention the ideal mother for his children. Neither the school nor her parents favored the marriage, at least not the first year, but the opposition only increased his Choleric resolve, and he pushed the matter determinedly until they marched down an aisle in July. He assumed responsibility for two jobs during the summer, and they returned to school in the fall.

Rocky decided to postpone the traditional honeymoon, so they married on Saturday night, drove 600 miles on

Sunday, and went to work on Monday. Within a few days Phlegmatic Phyllis realized that this whirling dervish of a husband was a perpetual motion machine. He loved her intensely, she admitted, but he loved work and activity even more. She found it almost impossible to sit him still long enough to smell the flowers and enjoy life. When she mildly protested that he seldom had time for her, he became defensive and would resort to sarcasm. She resorted to tears. Now she was forced to admit that she had no control over their lifestyle. Because he was such a rapid decision-maker, if she objected he would explode. Her only recourse was to crawl into her shell, clam up, and stubbornly dig in her heels.

Can you imagine the emotional tensions that built up during the "adjustment stage" (usually three years, but in their case more like 13 years)? Without realizing it, they had instituted a "push-pull" marriage—or as some label it, an "active-passive" relationship. As they entered the ministry—he determined and she stubbornly committed to "tough it out"—neither of them believed in divorce. It got tougher and tougher with each passing year and every new child until finally, in the providence of God, they discovered the secret of adjusting to their opposite temperaments, thereby transforming their marriage.

### Choleric Women Marry, Too!

Sarah was a Choleric. She was born that way. By the age of four she knew how to get the other kids in the neighborhood organized and motivated. Whatever she did, she was boss, and anyone who questioned her authority was quickly silenced. The business world would label her "a strong natural leader." When she met Ken, he was within a year of finishing medical school. A good-looking track star with a 4.0 grade point average, he felt somewhat insecure around the opposite sex and was much more confident about making it as a pathologist than in dating young women. So when Sarah came along, she easily led him into asking her out. They dated for two years, which she favored because she had to work diligently to maintain a high GPA during her final two years of college. Upon graduation, even though Ken had one more year of internship, she was ready to get married. Before he knew it, they had set the date and Sarah began planning the wedding.

She and her mother fought several skirmishes over wedding plans for a time, until her mother relented and let Sarah have her own way. That should have taught Ken something. But by this time he had fallen deeply in love with her and enjoyed letting her make all the decisions about both their present and future. When Sarah wanted to project herself as alluring, warm, and even sexy, she could turn on the charm—just so it served a good purpose, which was usually to get her own way. When Sarah wished, she could make Ken feel ten feet tall.

After they were married, Ken discovered that he barely had a minute to himself. If it weren't for his duties at the hospital, Sarah would have monopolized his every waking moment. Perhaps for that reason he found himself spending more time in the doctor's lounge at the hospital, the only quiet retreat in which to read the newspaper or pick up a book that interested him.

One Saturday he paid special attention to his bride's telephone conversation. As he clung to a ladder with one hand and attempted to clean the windows with the other, he overheard Sarah tell a friend, "My motto is, when you get him up—keep him moving!" Ken's eyes were suddenly opened. In response, he began to drag his feet, finding excuses not to heed Sarah's endless "honey-do list." But the more he stubbornly slowed his pace, the more she pushed, badgered, and attempted to manipulate him. When that failed, she exploded—at which point all her pent-up poisonous thoughts were voiced succinctly. Naturally, she felt badly after venting her anger, but Ken harbored his resentment and smoldered. (Ordinarily not given to violence, some phleg-matic men have been known to resort to it in a near-final attempt to be heard, and it is always harmful.)

Because Sarah was more articulate than he, Ken was always overmatched during their arguments. When she won, however, he saw to it that she lost by developing delaying tactics—which Sarah found maddening. When all else failed, he would just clam up. In fact, one time he went 21 days without speaking to her. As a result, Sarah sought counseling, which opened the door of marital adjustment to both of them. Today they are happily married—but it wasn't easy. If they forget to use the basic steps to adjust-ment, they immediately revert to their natural "push-pull" relationship.

## 3

OPPOSITES
*Attract*

# Who Wants
# a Cheerleader
# for a Wife?

Sally was the finest cheerleader in her college. With a sparkling personality and energy to burn, she was so pretty that everyone in the stadium responded to her enthusiastically. No one could work up a crowd better. Ned was captain of the football team and the middle linebacker. His impressive size kept the other fellows from coveting his girlfriend.

In college they enjoyed a life of endless activity. Ned considered this the result of his prominent position in sports, but in reality Sally's popularity caused them to be invited to a round of ceaseless activity. She was an endless talker, teaser, and joker, always the life of the party. Ned patiently listened to her repetitious flow of stories and cliches because being around her made him feel so good. He did become silently resentful when other men looked longingly at her, but he knew that in her heart she only had eyes for him. He did wish she wouldn't exaggerate so often, and he became embarrassed when she would announce, "Ned made ten unassisted tackles in Saturday's game"— when he had really only made eight!

Ned and Sally dated during all four years of college and married two weeks after graduation. Sally taught school as

Ned attended law school. Anyone who knew anything about temperament recognized their marriage was headed for trouble. In fact, discord began to simmer on their honeymoon. Returning to the hotel after an evening when his wife had been the life of the party, Ned remarked rather pointedly that she was very loose with her details. In essence, she had related the same story that evening that she had rehearsed to a different audience at their wedding party—but with conflicting particulars. Sally stared at him in amazement. "They laughed, didn't they?" she responded. Ned protested, "But it wasn't true!"

That difference may seem small to us, but over a lifetime it can be devastating. Ned told stories for accuracy; Sally narrated them for effect. In fact, many times Ned would refuse to tell a story if he didn't know the facts. Sally would proceed even if she had to create some details—just so she made the people laugh. "You're an old stick in the mud," she remonstrated. "You don't make anyone laugh, but you criticize me for the way I do it." They wounded each other's feelings so badly that they went to bed without making love—on their honeymoon! That was just the beginning of Ned trying to get Sally "in control"—which is nearly impossible without killing the spirit of a Sanguine.

Fun-loving Sally either stopped having fun around Ned to avoid his disapproval—for Sanguines can't stand criticism—or incurred his wrath every time she reverted to her talkative self. And once he started to criticize her public conversation, it didn't take long for him to censure almost everything she did. One day she became so upset that she exclaimed, "When are you ever going to stop trying to change me and accept me the way I am?"

One Sanguine I know who is married to a Melancholy became so angry during a honeymoon lover's quarrel that she took off her wedding ring in a fit of rage and threw it outside. "I don't want to be married to you anymore!" she raged. Later they made up, but when they searched in vain

for the ring, the analytical and creative Melancholy suggested, "Let's wait until dark—we'll find it with the flash-
light!" Sally thought he was crazy, forgetting that diamonds
glow when struck by light in the dark. Can you envision
those two reconciled lovebirds on their hands and knees in
the dark, poking around for their wedding ring—on their
honeymoon? After a variety of other explosions, they
learned to adjust to each other's differences. Today they
enjoy a very strong relationship—even though they are still
almost total opposites in temperament and personality.

# The Fun-Lover
# Who Married
# a Machine

Melancholies generally marry late in life, if at all. They are strong perfectionists by nature—usually quite bright, gifted, and creative. However, they frequently face a major hangup: "I can't find the perfect mate." And they never will. But they do have the capacity to love deeply while still being troubled by their fun-loving partner's obvious imperfections. Male Melancholies are vulnerable to the charms of their feminine companions, who can entice them to the altar if they tactfully refuse sexual satisfaction prior to marriage. Today's single women need to learn that "a realized need is a demotivator." If they surrender what a man needs sexually before the wedding, he is less likely to broach the subject of marriage. Besides, Melancholies often lose respect for the partner who submits sexually prior to marriage—even though both are participants.

Fortunately for Fred, Bonnie had too much Christian training and commitment to fall into that temptation, so he married her after a whirlwind courtship. Their honeymoon was thrilling, exciting, and very creative. Bonnie knew she had married the perfect man. He was 28 and she was 24; according to her testimony, "We were meant for each other." She had been teaching school for two years when Fred finished his internship and was hired on the staff of the local hospital. She was proud to be the wife of a young doctor who everyone said was destined for greatness. They were active in their church, and both were interested in starting a Christian home.

Fred lived by the book. He had a schedule for everything, never broke the speed limit, and always kept his closet in spotless condition—just the qualities one desires in a surgeon. But living with him 24 hours a day could be another matter. Sometimes he was moody and preoccupied. Fun-loving Bonnie had difficulty understanding why, after finishing medical school, he insisted on spending 15 percent of his time reading medical journals in order to "keep on the cutting edge" of his profession. Once a specialist learned how to remove certain organs, what else did he need to know? He might attend a medical convention occasionally, but that should be the extent of extracurricular involvement. Unfortunately, he insisted on being the best. He lived for tomorrow, while Bonnie lived for today. Many times they thought, "If I had known before we married how little we have in common, I never would have married you. You're a fine person, but we are total opposites."

All of these stories are true, representing the lives of personal friends who have found great help in the study of the four temperaments. Best of all, with God's help, they all enjoy strong marriages today. But like all opposite couples who marry, they had their moments.

# Why Do They Do It?

Most marriage counselors I know—and almost all proponents of various therapy styles—admit that in most marriages the old axiom is true, "Opposites attract each other"—at least in the Western world, where people choose their partners. The usual explanations of this phenomenon may contain certain elements of truth, but I have never been satisfied with any of them. So I devised my own.

Please read this chapter carefully. I will explain my theory at the outset, based on many years of study and the counseling of more than 6000 people, many for marital disharmony. Then I will describe the reasons behind my theory. Please wait until the end of the chapter before coming to your own conclusion.

## Likes Repel, Opposites Attract

In every field I know, from electricity to chemistry, pluses are attracted to negatives. In the human realm, introverts are usually attracted to extroverts. Admittedly, you and I can find exceptions, which explains why separating people into just two categories, as psychologists originally did, is inadequate. I can identify two kinds of introverts and two kinds of extroverts. In fact, in the next chapter, when we consider combinations of temperaments, I will introduce 12 different blends of temperament.

Basically, my theory contends that opposite temperaments of the opposite sex tend to attract each other, but to understand the concept more fully, we must take a brief look at human temperament. They don't realize it at the outset, but people are subconsciously attracted by the other person's strengths that correspond with their weaknesses.

## It's All in the Temperament

Twenty-five years ago I came to the conclusion that the most powerful single human influence on any person's behavior is his inherited temperament—or, more accurately stated, his combination of at least two temperaments, one primary and the other secondary. Since reaching that conclusion, I have pastored several thousand people, counseled more than 6000 individuals, conducted more than 700 Family Life Seminars in 46 countries of the world (attended by over one million people), written five books on the subject (read by at least four million people), and administered my LaHaye Temperament Test to more than 25,000 individuals—all of which further convinces me of the validity of the ancient theory of the four temperaments. It is not a perfect theory, but I believe it is the best explanation of human behavior ever developed by mortal man.

In embryo form it appears in the thirtieth chapter of Proverbs, where the writer identified four specific kinds of people. Agur, to whom many Bible scholars attribute the chapter, recognized these four kinds of people 500 years before Hippocrates (the father of modern medicine) gave names to them and began to classify them into this ancient theory. Keep in mind as you read the following verses that Agur only viewed them in their negative expressions, primarily because people are more easily diagnosed through their weaknesses than their strengths.

## Biblical Basis for Four Temperaments

### Agur—Proverbs 30 NASB

*Melancholy*
There is a kind of man who curses his father, and does not bless his mother (verse 11).

*Sanguine*
There is a kind—oh how lofty are his eyes! And his eyelids are raised in arrogance (verse 13).

*Phlegmatic*
There is a kind who is pure in his own eyes, yet is not washed from his filthiness (verse 12).

*Choleric*
There is a kind of man whose teeth are like swords, and his jaw teeth like knives, to devour the afflicted from the earth, and the needy from among men (verse 14).

## You're Born with It

Humanly speaking, nothing has a more profound influence on your behavior than your inherited temperament. The combination of your parents' genes and chromosomes at the time of conception determined your basic temperament nine months before you drew your first breath. That temperament combination is largely responsible for your actions, reactions, and emotional responses.

Most people are completely unaware of this extremely powerful influence on their behavior. Consequently, instead of cooperating with it and using it, they conflict with this inner power and often try to make something of themselves that they were never intended to be. This not only limits them personally but affects their immediate family and often spoils other interpersonal relationships. It is one reason so many people lament, "I don't like myself" or "I can't find myself." When a person discovers his own basic temperament, he can usually figure out rather easily what vocational opportunities he is best suited for, how to get along with other people, what natural weaknesses to watch for, what kind of wife he should marry, and how he can improve the effectiveness of his life.

## What Is Temperament?

Temperament is the combination of traits we inherited from our parents. No one knows where it resides, but it seems to be somewhere in the mind or emotional center (often referred to as the heart). From that source it combines with other human characteristics to produce our basic makeup. Most of us are more conscious of its *expression* than its function.

A person's temperament makes him outgoing and extroverted or shy and introverted. It impels some people to become art and music enthusiasts, whereas others are sports- or industry-minded. Children born of the same parents may have totally different temperaments; in fact, I have met outstanding musicians whose siblings were tone-deaf.

Temperament is not the only influence upon our behavior, of course. Early home life, training, education, sex, and motivation also exercise powerful influences on our actions throughout life. Temperament, however, dominates our life, not only because it affects us initially but because, like body structure, color of eyes, and other physical characteristics, it is permanent throughout life. An extrovert remains an extrovert. He may tone down the expression of his extroversion, but he will always be outgoing. Similarly, although an introvert may be able to come out of his shell and act more aggressively, he will never be transformed into an extrovert.

Temperament sets broad guidelines on everyone's behavior—patterns that will influence a person as long as he lives. On one side are his strengths, on the other his weaknesses. The primary advantage to learning about the four basic temperaments is to discover our most pronounced strengths and weaknesses so that with God's help we can overcome the weaknesses and take advantage of the strengths. In this way we can fulfill our personal destiny to the maximum.

Temperament, which is passed on through the genes, was no doubt influenced by the Adamic fall. That is why we all identify with the desire to do good while at the same time possessing an impulse to pursue evil. The apostle Paul no doubt felt that way when he declared, "For to will is present with me, but how to perform what is good I do not find. For the good that I will to do, I do not do; but the evil I will not to do, that I practice. Now if I do what I will not to do, it is no longer I who do it, but sin that dwells in me" (Romans 7:18-20).

Paul differentiated between himself and that uncontrollable force within him by asserting, "It is no longer I who do it, but sin that dwells in me." The "I" in Paul's person is the soul, will, and mind of man. The "sin" that dwelt in him was the human nature that he, like all human beings, inherited from his parents. Part of that human nature was his temperament. In his case, he was most likely a choleric-melancholy. And while the Holy Spirit made many improvements on his life, his strong-willed, determined brilliance was apparent all through his life.

The basic nature that we have all inherited from our parents is labeled in a variety of ways throughout Scripture: "the natural man," "the flesh," "the old man," and "corruptible flesh," to name a few. It provides the basic impulses of our being as we seek to satisfy our wants. To properly understand its control of our actions and reactions, we should distinguish carefully among temperament, character, and personality.

*Temperament* is the combination of inborn traits that subconsciously affect human behavior. These traits, arranged genetically on the basis of nationality, race, sex, and other hereditary factors, are passed on by the genes. Some psychologists suggest that we may get as many genes from our grandparents as we do from our parents, which could account for the greater resemblance of some children to their grandparents than to their parents. The alignment of temperament traits is just as unpredictable as the color of eyes or size of body.

*Character* is the real you. The Bible refers to it as "the hidden man of the heart." It is the result of your natural temperament modified by childhood training, education, and basic attitudes, beliefs, principles, and motivations. It is sometimes referred to as "the soul" of man, which is made up of the mind, emotions, and will.

*Personality* is the outward expression of ourselves, which may or may not be the same as our character, depending on how genuine we are. Often personality is a pleasing facade for an unpleasant or weak character. Many people are acting a part on the basis of what they think a person *should* be rather than on what they really are. This is a formula for mental and spiritual chaos. It is caused by following the human formula for acceptable conduct. The Bible tells us, "Man looks on the outward appearance, but God looks on the heart," and "Out of the heart proceed the issues of life." The place to change behavior is *inside* a person, not outside.

In summary, temperament is the combination of the traits we were born with; character is our "civilized" temperament; and personality is the "face" we show to others. Of the three, temperament has the greatest influence on our behavior.

During the past few years, many others have written and spoken on the temperament theory, both in the secular and Christian community. It has become popular for business and industrial psychologists, sales and management trainers, and, of course, success motivation speakers. Some, like Florence Littauer, refer to it as "personality." Gary Smalley has cleverly presented it in the form of different animals. But whatever it is called, it may be understood as the four temperaments.

Because I have written so much on the subject, I will forgo a detailed description of the temperaments here, providing just the simplest of definitions of the four types and referring you to the four books which you may read for added detail: *Spirit-Controlled Temperament* and *Why You Act the Way You Do,* published by Tyndale House Publishers; *Understanding the Male Temperament,* published by Revell Publishers; and for women my wife's book, *Spirit-Controlled Woman,* published by Harvest House. All of these are available through any of the 7000 Christian bookstores across the United States, and also in Canada and South America.

If you have not already met the four temperaments in one of the books mentioned above, consider these abbreviated descriptions of each temperament.

## The Sanguine

Sparky Sanguine is a warm, buoyant, lively, and "enjoying" person. He is receptive by nature, and external impressions easily find their way to his heart, where they readily cause an outburst of response. Feelings rather than reflective thoughts predominate to form his decisions. Sparky is so outgoing that I call him a superextrovert. Mr. Sanguine has an unusual capacity for enjoying himself and usually passes on his fun-loving personality. The moment he enters a room, he tends to lift the spirits of everyone present by his exuberant conversation. He is a fascinating storyteller, and his warm, emotional nature almost makes him relive the experience as he tells it.

Mr. Sanguine never lacks for friends. As one writer noted, "His naive, spontaneous, genial nature opens doors and hearts to him." He can genuinely feel the joys and sorrows of the person he meets and has the capacity to make him feel important, as though he were a very special friend—and he *is,* as long as Sparky is looking at him. He then moves to the next person he meets and fixes equal regard on him. The Sanguine has what I call "hanging eyes." That is, his eyes hang or "fix" on an individual until he loses interest or someone else comes along to attract his attention.

A Sanguine is never at a loss for words, though he often speaks without thinking. His open sincerity, however, has a disarming effect on many of his listeners, causing them to respond to his mood. His freewheeling, seemingly exciting, extrovertish way of life makes him the envy of the more timid temperament types.

Sparky Sanguine enjoys people and detests solitude. He is at his best surrounded by friends, serving as the life of the party. He provides an endless repertoire of interesting stories which he tells dramatically, making him a favorite with children as well as adults. This trait usually gains him admission at the best parties or social gatherings.

His noisy, blustering, friendly ways make him appear more confident than he really is, but his energy and lovable disposition get him by the rough spots of life. People have a way of excusing his weaknesses by saying, "That's just the way he is."

Like all temperaments, Sanguines have serious weaknesses, which, if left untended, will either destroy them or limit their incredible potential. Their greatest weakness, in my opinion, is reflected by a weak will and lack of discipline. Since they are highly emotional, exude considerable natural charm, and are prone to be what one psychologist called "touchers" (usually touching people as they talk to them), they commonly have a great appeal for the opposite sex. Consequently, they usually face more sexual temptation than others. Unfortunately, a weak will makes it easy for them to succumb to such temptations unless they are fortified by strong moral principles and possess a vital spiritual power.

This weakness of will and lack of discipline makes it easier for them to be deceitful, dishonest, and undependable. In addition, they tend to overeat and gain weight, finding it most difficult to remain on a diet; consequently, a 30-year-old Sanguine will often be 30 pounds overweight and gaining rapidly.

Someone has said, "Without self-discipline, there is no success." I couldn't agree more. Consider athletes, for example—no one is so gifted that he can excel without self-discipline. In fact, many a potential superstar has fizzled because he lacked it. On the other hand, an ordinary athlete has frequently excelled because he has disciplined himself, and others have prolonged their careers by "keeping their bodies under."

Lack of will and discipline are mentioned here first as we consider Mr. Sanguine's weaknesses because I am convinced that if he will conquer this tendency by the power of God, he will release an unlimited potential for good.

All temperaments have both strengths and weaknesses, pluses and minuses. Their talents and creativity come from their strengths. Weaknesses, of course, limit their natural potential. The success or failure of any temperament depends on the way in which the person overcomes his weaknesses. In a marriage relationship opposing weaknesses often collide, producing conflict. However, among the very selfish, a partner's strengths can also be a source of discontent.

## Sanguine Strengths and Weaknesses

This fun-loving, people-oriented person is a natural salesman, con artist, or people manipulator. No one has a more natural gift to motivate and work with others—if he can get his act together. Although he primarily lacks self-discipline, other weaknesses also arise, as the following chart indicates:

| *Strengths* | *Weaknesses* |
|---|---|
| Warm emotionally | Lacking in discipline |
| Friendly | Weak-willed |
| Fun-loving | Egotistical |
| Outgoing-extrovertish | Emotionally excitable |
| Enthusiastic | Unstable |
| Talkative | Prone to exaggerate |
| Compassionate | Hot-tempered |
| Responsive | Disorganized |
| Stimulating | Manipulative |
| Ambitious | Restless |

This "high-assertive/high-responsive" person is born with good interpersonal skills. If he can overcome his weaknesses and learn to be dependable and consistent, there is no limit to his potential.

## The Choleric

Rocky Choleric is the hot, quick, active, practical, strong-willed temperament type who is self-sufficient and very independent. He tends to be decisive and opinionated, finding it easy to make decisions both for himself and other people. Like Sparky Sanguine, Rocky Choleric is an extrovert, but not nearly so intense.

Mr. Choleric thrives on activity. In fact, to him life is activity. He does not need to be stimulated by his environment, but stimulates his environment with his endless ideas, plans, goals, and ambitions. He rarely engages in aimless activity, for he has a practical, keen mind, capable of making sound, instant decisions and planning worthwhile projects. Never vacillating under the pressure of what others think, he takes a firm stand on issues and can often be found crusading against some social injustice or subversive activity.

Rocky is not frightened by adversity; in fact, it tends to encourage him. His dogged determination usually allows him to succeed where others have failed, not because his plans are better than theirs, but because others have become discouraged and quit, whereas he has doggedly kept pushing ahead. If there is any truth to the adage that leaders are born, not made, then he is a born leader, identified by business management experts as "the SNL" (Strong Natural Leader).

Mr. Choleric's emotional nature is the least-developed part of his temperament. He does not sympathize easily with others, nor does he naturally show or express compassion. He is often embarrassed or disgusted by the tears of others and is usually insensitive to their needs. Reflecting little appreciation for music or the fine arts, unless his secondary temperament traits are those of the Melancholy, he primarily seeks utilitarian and productive values in life.

Rocky Choleric would be an engaging person were it not for his very serious weaknesses, chief among them being anger. Cholerics are extremely hostile people. Some learn to control their anger, but most remain dormant volcanoes, threatening a violent eruption. If their strong will is not brought into control by proper parental discipline as children, they develop angry, tumultuous habits that plague them throughout life. It doesn't take them long to learn that other people are usually afraid of their angry outbursts, and so they use their wrath as a weapon to get what they want—which is usually *their own way*.

The anger of Cholerics is quite different from that of Sanguines. Rocky's explosion is seldom as loud as Sparky's because he is not quite as extrovertish as the Sanguine, but it can be much more dangerous. Sanguines have a gentle streak that makes it difficult for them to injure other people purposely (although they can bruise them thoughtlessly). Not so with a Choleric. With determined malice he may willfully cause pain to others and enjoy it. His wife is usually afraid of him, and he tends to terrify his children.

Rocky Choleric often reminds me of a walking Mount Vesuvius, constantly smoking and rumbling until, at a moment of provocation, he spews out his poisonous or bitter lava all over someone or something. He is a door-slammer, table-pounder, and horn-blower. Any person who gets in his way, retards his progress, or fails to perform up to the level of his expectations will soon feel the eruption of his wrath. Unlike the Sanguine, who usually vents his anger but cools down rather quickly, Rocky may carry a grudge for an unbelievably long time. Maybe that's why he often falls prey to ulcers by the time he is 40 years old.

No one utters more acrid comments than a sarcastic Choleric! Sometimes we wonder whether he inherited a tongue or a razor blade. As an extrovert, he is usually ready with a cutting remark that can wither the insecure and devastate the less combative. Even Sparky Sanguine is no match for him because Sparky is neither cruel nor mean. Rocky will rarely hesitate to scorch his adversary with a scathing attack. Consequently, he leaves a path of damaged psyches and fractured egos wherever he goes.

It is a happy Choleric (and his family members) who discovers that the tongue is either a vicious weapon of destruction or a tool of healing. Once he learns the importance of verbal approval and encouragement, he will seek to control his speech—until he gets angry, whereupon he discovers with the apostle James that "no man can tame the tongue. It is an unruly evil, full of deadly poison" (James 3:8). Ready speech and an angry spirit often unite to make a Choleric extraordinarily profane. His language is not only improper for female company but often unfit for man or beast.

The milk of human kindness has all but dried up in the veins of a Choleric. He is the most unaffectionate of all the temperaments and becomes emotionally spastic at the thought of any public show of emotion. Marital affection to him means a kiss at the wedding and on every fifth anniversary thereafter. Except for anger, his emotions are the most underdeveloped of all the temperaments. As the wife of a Choleric for 24 years lamented in the counseling room, "My husband is terribly cold and unaffectionate. He lets me use his lips, but there is never any real feeling to it. Kissing him is about as exciting as kissing a marble statue in a cemetery on a cold winter day!"

The Rocky Cholerics of this life are very effective people if their weaknesses are not indulged. When they are filled with the Spirit, their tendencies toward willfulness and harshness are supplanted by a gentleness which verifies clearly that they are controlled by something other than their own natural temperament. From the days of the apostle Paul until the present, both the church of Jesus Christ and society have benefited greatly from these active, productive people. Many of our major church institutions were founded by venturous Cholerics. But to be effective in God's service, they must learn the divine principles of productivity: "Not by [Choleric] might nor by [natural] power, but by *My Spirit,* says the Lord of hosts" (Zechariah 4:6).

## Choleric Strengths and Weaknesses

The active, hard-driving and productive Choleric makes a good leader and employee—but in voluntary relationships, he or she can be extremely volatile.

| *Strengths* | *Weaknesses* |
| --- | --- |
| Strong-willed | Unemotional and cold |
| Determined | Self-sufficient |
| Independent | Impetuous |
| Decisive | Domineering |
| Active and energetic | Unforgiving |
| Practical | Hostile and volatile |
| Strong natural leader | Sarcastic and cruel |
| Optimistic and confident | Impatient |
| Productive | Unsympathetic |
| Goal-oriented | Opinionated |

The success of this "high-assertive/low-responsive" person will be determined by how well he or she overcomes weaknesses and learns to work with other people. He does not possess natural interpersonal skills—he must learn them. Some behavior experts call him "driver-driver" or "active-assertive," as the above verifies.

## The Melancholy

Martin Melancholy is the richest of all the temperaments—an analytical, self-sacrificing, gifted, perfectionist type with a very sensitive emotional nature. No one gets more enjoyment from the fine arts than the Melancholy. By nature he is prone to be an introvert, but since his feelings predominate, he is given to a variety of moods. Sometimes they will lift him to heights of ecstasy that cause him to act more extroverted. However, at other times he will be gloomy and depressed, and during these periods he becomes withdrawn and can be quite antagonistic. This tendency toward black moods has earned him the reputation of being the "dark temperament."

Martin is a very faithful friend, but unlike the Sanguine, he does not make friends easily. He seldom pushes himself forward to meet people, but rather lets them come to him. He is perhaps the most dependable of all the temperaments, for his perfectionist tendencies do not permit him to be a shirker or let others down when they are counting on him. His natural reticence to put himself forward is not an indication that he doesn't enjoy people. Like the rest of us, he not only likes others but has a strong desire to be loved by them. Disappointing experiences, however, make him reluctant to take people at face value; he is prone to be suspicious when others seek him out or shower him with attention.

His exceptional analytical ability causes him to diagnose accurately the obstacles and dangers of any project he has a part in planning. This is in sharp contrast to the Choleric, who rarely anticipates problems or difficulties, but is confident he can cope with whatever crises may arise. Such a characteristic often finds the Melancholy reticent to initiate some new project, or he may conflict with those who wish to do so. Whenever a person looks at obstacles instead of resources or goals, he will easily become discouraged before he starts. If one confronts a Melancholy about his pessimistic state, he will usually retort, "I am not being negative! I'm just being realistic." In other words, his usual thinking process makes him realistically pessimistic. Occasionally, in one of his exemplary moods of emotional ecstasy or inspiration, he may produce some great work of art, but such accomplishments are often followed by periods of intense depression. Some of the world's greatest geniuses have been notorious for their long bouts of melancholia. And some have even committed suicide.

Martin Melancholy usually finds his greatest meaning in life through personal sacrifice. He seems to enjoy making himself suffer, and will often choose a difficult life vocation involving sacrifice. But once it is chosen, he is prone to be exceptionally thorough and persistent in his pursuit of it, and he will accomplish great good if his natural tendency to gripe throughout the sacrificial process doesn't get him so depressed that he gives up on it altogether. No temperament has so much natural potential when energized by the Holy Spirit.

The creativity and innate strengths of the Melancholy are as pronounced as his weaknesses. For example, the admirable qualities of perfectionism and conscientiousness are often interwoven with the spirit of negativism, pessimism, and criticism. Anyone who has worked with a gifted Melancholy very long can anticipate that his first reaction to anything will be negative. Melancholies in our college and church organizations instinctively respond "Impossible!" "It won't work!" "It can't be done!" "We've tried that once and failed!" "The people will never go for it!" That final generalization is particularly aggravating, for the reference usually applies only to the Melancholy who is raising the objection!

The most damaging influence upon a person's mind, in my opinion, is criticism; thus the Melancholy has to fight that spirit constantly. He suffers from negative thoughts, but then he compounds the problem by verbalizing them, which not only reinforces the spirit of negation but devastates his wife, children, and friends. He is endlessly examining his spiritual life and coming up short—in his own mind—despite the fact that he is most likely to be more devoted than others. As one Melancholy fretted, "I've confessed all the sins I can remember, but I know there must be others that I just can't recall." This kept him from enjoying any confidence with God.

## Melancholy Strengths and Weaknesses

The gifted Melancholy temperament, whether male or female, is the broadest and richest of all temperaments but reflects the most weaknesses. No temperament offers more potential but falls far below expectations due to negative mood swings and lack of self-confidence.

| Strengths | Weaknesses |
|---|---|
| Gifted | Moody |
| Analytical | Deeply emotional |
| Perfectionist | Easily offended |
| Self-disciplined | Pessimistic |
| Industrious | Negative |
| Self-sacrificing | Critical and picky |
| Aesthetic | Theoretical and impractical |
| Creative | Suspicious and revengeful |
| Sensitive | Self-centered |
| Loyal and faithful | Indecisive |

These "low-assertive/high-responsive" people must be motivated externally—by God, others, or projects. It is difficult for them to remain idle, for when they are not motivated by others they turn introspective and begin to psychoanalyze themselves, thereby destroying their self-confidence. Many of the most outstanding servants of God have been Melancholies who were filled with the Spirit. All the prophets were Melancholy, as were Moses and several of the faithful apostles and disciples of our Lord. The Melancholy can fulfill his potential only through the Spirit-filled life (Ephesians 5:17-21), which causes him to become a thankful praiser instead of a gloomy griper!

## The Phlegmatic

Philip Phlegmatic is the calm, easygoing, never-get-upset individual with such a high boiling point that he seldom becomes angry. He is without question the easiest person to get along with and is by nature the most likable of all the temperaments.

He derives his name from the body fluid "phlegm," which according to Hippocrates produced that calm, cool, slow, well-balanced temperament. Life for him is a mellow, pleasant experience in which he avoids as much involvement as possible. He is so calm and unruffled that he never seems agitated, no matter what circumstances surround him. He is consistent every time you see him. However, beneath his cool, reticent, almost timid personality, Mr. Phlegmatic has a very capable combination of abilities. He feels much more emotion than appears on the surface and has the capacity to appreciate the fine arts and the better things of life.

The Phlegmatic does not lack for friends, because he enjoys people and has a natural, dry sense of humor. He is the type of individual who can have a crowd of people in stitches, yet never crack a smile. Possessing the unique capability for seeing something humorous in others and their action, he maintains a positive approach to life. He has a retentive mind and is capable of being a fine imitator. He regularly delights in "needling" or poking fun at the other temperament types. For instance, he is annoyed by the aimless, restless enthusiasm of the Sanguine and disgusted by the gloomy moods of the Melancholy. The former, says Mr. Phlegmatic, must be confronted with his futility, the latter with his morbidity. He relishes an opportunity to throw icewater on the bubbling plans and ambitions of the Choleric.

Phil Phlegmatic tends to be a spectator in life and tries not to get very involved with the activities of others. In fact, with great reluctance is he ever motivated to any form of activity beyond his daily routine. When once aroused to action, however, his capable and efficient qualities become apparent. He will not volunteer for leadership on his own, but when it is forced upon him, he proves to be a very capable leader. He has a conciliating effect on others and acts as a natural peacemaker.

In spite of his nice-guy image and easygoing temperament, the Phlegmatic is not perfect. But then, what temperament is? The most obvious of Phil Phlegmatic's weaknesses—and that which caused Hippocrates to label him phlegm, slow or sluggish—is his apparent lack of drive and ambition. Although he always seems to do the expected, he will rarely exceed the status quo. One almost feels that his metabolism is low, his blood "thick"; he frequently falls asleep the moment he sits down. Rarely does he instigate an activity, preferring to concoct excuses in order to avoid getting involved with the activities of others, and his engine tends to decelerate with each passing year.

One of the less obvious weaknesses of the Phlegmatic is his selfishness. Every temperament faces this problem, but Phil is particularly afflicted with the disease, though he is so gracious and proper that few people are aware of it. Self-ishness makes him self-indulgent and unconcerned about his family's need for activity. Nowhere is his selfishness more apparent than in his use of money. He is a penny pincher and a miser except where clothes for himself or tools for his work are concerned.

No one can be more stubborn than a Phlegmatic, but he is so diplomatic that he may proceed halfway through life before others catch on. He almost never openly confronts another person or refuses to do something—but he will somehow manage to sidestep the demand.

In family situations, Phlegmatics never yell or argue—they just drag their feet or refuse to budge. They often remind me of the Missouri mule that stubbornly refuses the urgings of his master. Pushing or pulling will avail nothing. Sometimes we are tempted to slip a stick of dynamite under them.

While Phlegmatics never make waves, they can be exasperating to a more aggressive partner by their passive, laid-back lifestyle. This is a widespread problem, as illustrated by the inquiry I received from six wives during the question period at one of my recent Family Seminars. They wrote, "How do you motivate a Phlegmatic husband?" Very honestly, it's difficult. For as in all weaknesses (as we will see in a later chapter), without the help of the individual himself, it is all but impossible to get any temperament to improve his natural weaknesses. Even then, he needs God's help. But it can be done!

## Phlegmatic Strengths and Weaknesses

These nice, gentle people, who often act more like Christians before they accept Christ than some of the rest of us after our conversion, are far from perfect. They are just more polite and diplomatic about the expression of their old sin nature. One of their chief weaknesses is motivation—they have very little.

| Strengths | Weaknesses |
|---|---|
| Calm, cool | Passive and unmotivated |
| Easygoing | Subject to procrastination |
| Diplomatic | Indecisive |
| Dependable | Fearful and filled |
| Objective | with worry |
| Efficient | Unsure |
| Orderly | Self-protective |
| Practical | Stubborn |
| Humorous | Selfish |
| Agreeable | Stingy |
| | Slow and lazy |

These "low-assertive/low-responsive" people are usually superintroverts who like to stay in the background and work at their own pace, which diminishes with each passing year.

## Summary

Well, there you have it—an abbreviated look at the four temperaments. The above introduction should help you understand the four basic temperament styles in preparation for the explanation as to why opposites attract each other.

# 6
## OPPOSITES
### *Attract*

# Likes Repel,
# Opposites Attract

In all the years I have been counseling, I have never seen two people of the same temperament get married. While such an event must have taken place among the five billion people on planet Earth, I have never met one. In analyzing the couples who have taken my temperament test, 89 percent could clearly be identified as opposites and the other 11 percent had significant areas of difference. People who think they are married to a mate of the same temperament either don't understand the temperaments, have made an improper diagnosis, or have forgotten that all of us have at least two temperaments, a primary and a secondary. But more of that in the next chapter.

We tend to like people of our own temperament only in short doses. For instance, two fun-loving Sanguines might date each other, but it would be an exhausting experience emotionally, for each would be trying one-upmanship on the other for the entire evening. No one has enough emotion to last a lifetime like that.

Shakespeare said it best: To the Sanguine, "all the world's a stage!" Sanguines are performers, which is why they marry spectators. Other Sanguines are a threat to them. As any actor will tell you, it's no fun to perform without an audience which responds with applause. Can you imagine two Sanguines looking to each other for approval? They wouldn't do it for very long—usually not long enough to marry.

And I'm even more certain that two Cholerics would never marry. In fact, they probably wouldn't venture out on a single date. Can you imagine two opinionated, aggressive, sarcastic people, each accustomed to making decisions, trying to determine where to go, where to eat, and who should pay? They would probably start an argument before they even backed out of the lady Choleric's driveway. Dating doubtful—marriage never!

Two Phlegmatics might date each other, but they would go together, and gooo tooogether, and gooooo toooogether for many years. One would probably die of old age before either built up enough steam to ask the other to marry. No, as a general rule, Phlegmatics sit around waiting for the more forceful person to pursue the relationship. Usually that is a Choleric.

However, if one temperament *might* marry its own kind, it would be a Melancholy. If both settled into a sadistic mood for a long enough period of time, they might pursue marriage—but it is most unlikely. Quite frankly, if a perfectionist goes with a person long enough, he will find something about the prospective partner that he can criticize; and if criticism, expressed or thought, is indulged long enough, it will kill love, before or after marriage.

As a general rule, Melancholies are attracted to the more charismatic Sanguine types who are prone to sweep them off their feet, rush them to the altar, and marry them before they begin to suspect the partner's flaws. Then it is too late, at least for Christians, for whom divorce is not the answer.

## Opposites Attract Each Other

A young engineer who came in for counseling spent the first 25 minutes of our interview complaining about his wife. Then he buried his face in his hands and groaned, "I just can't understand why I married that woman in the first place." Here was a man who was so crazy about a beautiful young woman just four years earlier that he couldn't work, sleep, or play without thinking about her. Actually, he was still thinking about her—but on a different wavelength. Before marriage he was filled to overflowing with thoughts of love; four years later his critical thoughts had decimated his romantic feelings and were eating him alive.

The answer to his question "Why did I marry her?" is rather clear. During their courtship he only perceived the good side of her, the strengths. That is usually all that any of us see in our partner *before* marriage. Why? Two reasons: Love is blind, and, like all other human beings in a dating situation, she always put her best foot forward. Not meaning to be hypocritical, she was responding to him positively as a matter of social survival! If any of us projected our true self socially, we would not find anyone foolish enough to marry us. Instead, we display ourselves as attractively as we can, only revealing our strengths. That is why . . .

## Sanguines Attract Melancholies

As a general rule, fun-loving Sanguines are drawn to somber Melancholies, and Melancholies respond best to uninhibited Sanguines. Mr. or Miss Melancholy is a listener, and as we have seen, Sanguines need a spectator to appreciate their irrepressible showmanship. Melancholies are organized, capable people who subconsciously possess the qualities that Mr. Sanguine knows are missing in his life. By contrast, the Melancholy is aware that he is susceptible to morose introspection and depression, and thus needs someone to bring joy into his life. Sanguines, male or female, are gifted at doing that, for they are natural-born cheerleaders, lifting the spirits of the Melancholy. Given enough exposure, the vivacious Sanguine becomes a narcotic to the Melancholy emotions. Eventually the Melancholy becomes dependent on his counterpart to sustain a buoyant, joyful quality of life.

It is the contrasting strengths of these two people that have brought them together.

## Cholerics Attract Phlegmatics

Activity-generating Cholerics are attracted to easygoing Phlegmatic followers. Cholerics are forceful, Phlegmatics passive. Therefore they need each other. The Phlegmatic requires someone to pursue the relationship, and the Choleric desires someone to pursue.

The dynamic, whirling-dervish Choleric somehow feels comfortable around that gentle Phlegmatic spirit, which doesn't threaten his control of the relationship. Many have declared, "I just feel so relaxed around him" (before marriage, that is). By contrast, the Phlegmatic, who often gets bored with his own company or lack of involvement, is just waiting for someone to come along and encourage or challenge him to do something. No one can motivate to activity better than the Choleric—and that is true of both sexes. A Choleric woman just intuitively knows how to motivate a Phlegmatic male before marriage (much more tactfully than after marriage, I might add). She, like her male counterpart, can move in with a capacity for fun and games that brings real pleasure to the person who naturally wants to follow. Again, the contrasting temperaments complement one another.

## 7

OPPOSITES
*Attract*

# *How It Works*

We are subconsciously attracted to the strengths of our opposite partner because they correspond with our weaknesses. When we see a person with our own temperament, abilities, and talents, we are not overly impressed, for we all take our strengths more or less for granted. The people who impress us most are those who demonstrate strength in areas where we are weak.

Consequently, when we meet someone of the opposite temperament and sex, within a reasonable age span and philosophy of our own, we are impressed positively. This can lead to infatuation, which usually propels us into additional associations. Given enough exposure, opposites may progress into a love relationship, and for most people, love leads to marriage.

## Marriage—That's the Rub!

Emerson, the humanistic poet-philosopher of an earlier generation, described love as "an emotion that ends with marriage." I am more positive about that God-ordained institution, believing that marriage opens the door (or can) to the most sublime relationship two people can share on this earth. But it will take adjustment on the part of both partners.

Marriage is a disclosure. When two people stand before the preacher and pledge their faithfulness before God and their invited witnesses, they are promising, "I will love and cherish you for as long as we both shall live." In essence, they are affirming, "Because I accept your pledge of love and devotion, I will reveal myself totally to you—not only physically but also psychologically. Until this time I have only revealed my strengths. Now that we are married, I can expose my total self to you, and I have faith in your commitment that you will love me just the same."

My dear friend and Christian psychologist Dr. Henry Brandt used to say when we did Family Life Seminars together, "There is no nakedness comparable to psychological nakedness!" And that is the rub. Marriage is not all sweetness and light; it is the revelation of the other side of your partner's nature—his weaknesses. What may have remained hidden in the personality will now come forth into the light, which may put love's commitment to its ultimate test.

## The Advantage of Premarital Virtue

Right here I must insert a biblical bias—that of maintaining virtue until marriage. I am fully aware of the humanistic statisticians who suggest that "70 percent of all young people engage in premarital sex today." Personally, I am dubious of their statistics, for 1) humanistic relativists like to falsify facts to promote their own relativistic agenda; 2) their assessment may not include active Christians; and 3) they lump the sexually promiscuous together with those young people who have experienced only one or two liaisons early in life but are determined not to repeat the practice and have had no sexual contact with the person they eventually marry. Certainly, the grim fact of the highest divorce rate existing among those who have lived together sexually before marriage indicates that virtue and morality do indeed have their own reward.

From a practical perspective regarding the adjustment stage of newlyweds (which most counselors estimate lasts from three to seven years), I am of the persuasion that happy adjustments are much higher among those who determinedly kept themselves from sexual activity with each other prior to marriage. Sexual expression among inexperienced newlyweds is so exciting that it can ease them through those adjustment days with a minimum of conflict in spite of the revelation of differences, particularly weaknesses. When the one person on earth with whom you can express your sexual needs can bring such pleasure to you, it reduces the revelation of human weaknesses in other areas to manageable size. By the time youthful sexual ecstasy subsides a bit, both partners have matured, "know their partner," and love him anyway. As we shall see, one of the keys to a quick and lasting adjustment is to concentrate on a partner's strengths throughout marriage and avoid focusing on his weaknesses!

## Why Do People Marry, Anyway?

Lest you think all this is unrealistic idealism, ask yourself why people marry in the first place. It certainly is not easier or cheaper than living alone. But when the issues are examined in their entirety, we marry because we have basic needs that cannot be fulfilled by living independently. Just as Adam when living in the midst of the Garden of Eden, the most magnificent environment ever created on earth, was not complete or fulfilled until God created a special mate for him, neither are we moderns.

Our most important needs can be satisfied only by a person of the opposite sex. We require intimate companionship, sexual expression, a nest of our own, the comfort and delight of children—and the list goes on. Few would disagree that couples need each other. Evidence comes to us in the high number of divorcees (or those left by death) who eventually seek out someone else with whom to share their life. That is the way God made us; after 6000 years of human history, marriage always has been and still is the number one relationship shared by the vast majority of people. No other relationship even comes close.

The fact that opposites attract each other, not only socially but temperamentally, should not disillusion or discourage us about this God-ordained relationship. To the contrary, it should inspire us as we seek His help in adjusting to our partner. I like to think that marrying the opposite temperament is an asset, not a liability. Two people of opposing temperaments who learn to accept and adjust to each other will accomplish much more together than either of them could separately. The complementary differences of the sexes is a tangible, positive illustration of the benefit enjoyed by total opposites.

## 8

# *Opposite Temperament Blends*

During the 25 years that I have helped to popularize the theory of the four temperaments in this country, I have made two contributions to the field that still seem unique to me. First and most important is the way in which the Holy Spirit of God, after a person's conversion, can help strengthen his or her weaknesses so that the natural strengths of temperament can enable him to fulfill his potential. Second, I have advocated the principle that no one is 100 percent a single temperament, but that we are all a combination of temperaments. We represent at least two temperaments, and some people, according to the thousands of tests I have administered, are three temperaments—one primary and two secondary temperaments.

Every human being can identify six people who, through the genes at the time of conception, contributed to his physical and temperament makeup—two parents and four grandparents. That is why a child will occasionally look nothing like his parents but will favor one of his grandparents. The same is true of temperament. It is important to note that temperament has nothing to do with the date of a person's birth, but everything to do with the date of conception. A person's temperament is arranged by God at the fall of the genes during the process of conception. What he is in the womb becomes what he is in life. I have interviewed enough mothers to confirm that "a kicker in the womb is a kicker in life." Similarly, a passive, docile child in the womb will usually be an easygoing child in life.

For this reason I have never paid much attention to critics who try to accuse me of propounding a theory that is based on the horoscope. That heresy is predicated on the day of a person's birth, not on the time of conception. Even if the stars had anything to do with our behavior, the predictability factor would be totally unreliable because it would be nine months off the charts. Conception was the most important day of your life, for on that day you became a living person with an eternal soul, a free will, a temperament combination, and the embryonic potential to pass on that priceless gift to your children. But to do that you must have a mate—an opposite partner who is both complementary to and compatible with your needs. And that is what this book is about.

It would be much simpler to report, as the ancients taught, that only four temperaments exist. While I agree that one of the four dominates in each individual's personality, we all have a secondary temperament that to one extent or another influences our behavior. When the writer of Proverbs, and later Hippocrates, first noticed the four temperaments, the races were more separated and confined so people tended to reflect only one basic category. Today, however, nationalities and races have been so commingled that no one is 100 percent one temperament. Most people test out predominantly 55 to 70 percent one temperament with a secondary that runs anywhere from 30 to 45 percent. Take my wife and me, for example. I am Scotch, French, and Irish; she is Welsh and Scotch. Obviously, at least four distinct nationalities influences and contributes to our makeup, which produces my temperament of Choleric-Sanguine and hers of Phlegmatic-Sanguine (with a tad of Melancholy).

## A Psychiatrist Confirms the Blends

During the year of sabbatical leave from our pastorate in San Diego, my wife and I visited 46 countries of the world to conduct our Family Life Seminars for missionaries. When a psychiatrist in Sydney, Australia, heard that we were coming to his city, he arranged in advance to take me to lunch. "I have something important to tell you," he said.

After we enjoyed the view of the exquisitely beautiful Sydney harbor, he proceeded to explain that he was an expert in Lucher Color testing. He had flown to London on several occasions to take special training in the field and had used it extensively in the assessment of his patients. It seems that there are 12 colors which upon testing reveal each one of the temperaments. Each person tested ended with a blend of colors making 12 possibilities, corresponding to the 12 blends of temperament.

Taking a well-worn copy of *Understanding the Male Temperament,* which I didn't realize had already reached Australia, he turned to Chapter 6 and said, "After I have diagnosed a person's temperament combination based on his color preferences, I then turn to the corresponding temperament explanation that you give in this book and read him your description of that temperament combination. Almost invariably he will respond by saying, 'That man is describing me perfectly. That's the way I am!'"

More research should be done on this, of course, but it is interesting that color testing can reveal temperament combinations. This should not surprise us, for temperament influences almost everything we do or choose, including our natural preferences for colors. But I am fascinated that the four-color test of people works out to 12 blends that correlates with the blends of temperament.

We are all a blend of at least two temperaments; one predominates, the other is secondary. There are also some people who seem to possess three temperaments, one that predominates and two that are secondary.

In an attempt to make the temperament theory more practical and true to life, we shall briefly examine the 12 possible blends of temperament. In all probability, it will be easier for you to identify yourself in one of the blends than in only one of the four basics.

One salient factor should be kept in mind when considering blends—not all of the same degree. For example, a person who is 60 percent Sanguine/40 percent Choleric will be somewhat different from the person who is 80 percent Sanguine/20 percent Choleric. Consequently, some variables will exist even within these blends. For clarity's sake, I will not attempt to break the temperaments down into more than the 12 blends but shall use 60 percent for the predominant temperament and 40 percent for the secondary temperament.

## The San-Chlor

The strongest extrovert of all the blends of temperaments is the San-Chlor, for the two temperaments that make up his nature are both extroverts. The happy charisma of the Sanguine makes him a people-oriented, enthusiastic, salesperson type, but the Choleric side of his nature will provide him the necessary resolution and character traits that will fashion a somewhat more organized and productive individual than if he were pure Sanguine. Vocationally, this person often starts out in sales or promotion and ends up as sales manager of the company. Almost any people-oriented field is open to him, but to sustain his interest it must offer variety, activity, and excitement. He is invariably a sports enthusiast. Ordinarily, such an individual is financially successful in life if properly trained and motivated and loved by his family, and when not controlled by his weaknesses. His financial success is usually tied to his ability (or training) to learn how to discipline his spending. Good salespeople are often vulnerable to other sales-people. They have no sales resistance and the more they make the more they spend. Consequently, they can make several fortunes in a lifetime—and lose them all.

The potential weaknesses of a San-Chlor are usually apparent to everyone because he is such an external person. He custom-arily talks too much, thus exposing himself and his weaknesses for all to see. He is highly opinionated. Con-sequently, he expresses himself loudly even before he knows all the facts. No one has more mouth trouble! I was amused when a nationally known San-Chlor evangelist visited our city and was dubbed by the news-paper as "the fastest lip in the West." His giant ego so dominated his conversation that he often destroyed the good first impression he made and did not wear well. If he sensed that people resisted him, he tended to come on even stronger and make matters worse. I was saddened but not surprised to see him blow his min-istry by overspending and eventually committing adultery.

If the San-Chlor is the life of the party, he is lovable, but if he feels threatened or insecure, he can become obnox-ious. His leading emotional problem will be anger, which can catapult him into action at the slightest provocation. Ego is a strong factor in his driving activity. The San-Chlor can be complimentary when it suits his purpose, but if you cross him, he may cut you down. Since he combines the easy forgetfulness of the Sanguine and the diligent ratio-nalization of the Choleric, he may not have an active con-science. Consequently, he tends to justify his actions, often rationalizing that the law applies to everyone else. This person, like any other temperament, needs to be filled with the Holy Spirit and the Word of God daily!

Simon Peter, the self-appointed leader of the 12 apostles, is a classic example of a New Testament San-Chlor. He obviously had mouth trouble, demonstrating this repeatedly by speaking up before anyone else could. He talked more in the gospels than all the other put together—and most of what he said was wrong. He was egotistical, weak-willed, and carnal throughout the gospels. In Acts, however, he was a remarkably transformed man, resolute, effective, and productive. What made the difference? He had become filled with the Spirit.

## The San-Mel

San-Mels are highly emotional people who fluctuate drastically. They can laugh hysterically one minute and burst into tears the next. It is almost impossible for them to hear a sad tale, observe the tragic plight of another person, or listen to melancholy music without weeping profusely. They genuinely feel the griefs of others. San-Mel doctors, for instance, always display the best bedside manner. Ordinarily they make fantastic instructors, teachers, and college professors—and are easily the most popular instructors on campus. Almost any field is open to them, especially public speaking, acting, music, and the fine arts. However, San-Mels reflect an uninhibited perfectionism that often alienates them from others because they verbalize their criticisms. They are usually people-oriented individuals who have sufficient substance to make a contribution to other lives—if their egos and arrogance don't make them so obnoxious that others become hostile to them.

One of the crucial weaknesses of this temperament blend prevails in his thought life. Both Sanguines and Melancholies are dreamers, and thus if the Melancholy part of his nature suggests a negative train of thought, it can nullify a San-Mel's potential. It is easy for him to get down on himself. In addition, this person, more than most others, will have both an anger problem and a tendency toward fear. Both temperaments in his makeup are prone to insecurity; not uncommonly, the San-Mel is afraid to utilize his potential. Such a person should always work with people. Being admired by others is so important to him that it will drive him to a consistent level of performance. Of all Sanguine public speakers, the San-Mel will be most accurate in his statistics and organized in his presentation. He has a great ability to commune with God, and if he walks in the Spirit, he will make an effective servant of Christ.

King David is a classic illustration of the San-Mel temperament. An extremely likable man who attracted both men and women (charisma), he was colorful, dramatic, emotional, and weak-willed. He could play a harp and sing, he clearly demonstrated a poetic instinct in his psalms, and he made decisions on impulse. Unfortunately, like many San-Mels, he fouled up his life by a series of disastrous and costly mistakes before he gained enough self-discipline to finish out his destiny. Not all San-Mels, of course, are able to pick up the pieces of their lives and start over, as David did. It is far better for them to walk in the Spirit daily and avoid such mistakes.

## The San-Phleg

The easiest person to like is the San-Phleg. The overpowering and obnoxious tendencies of a Sanguine are offset by the gracious, easygoing Phlegmatic, so the charisma possessed by all Sanguines makes him a delightful

associate. San-Phlegs are extremely happy people whose carefree spirit and good humor make them light-hearted entertainers sought after by others. Helping people is their regular business, along with sales of various kinds. They are the least extroverted of any of the Sanguines and are often regulated by their environment and circumstances rather than being self-motivated. San-Phlegs are naturally good family people and preserve the love of their children—and everyone else for that matter. They would not purposely hurt anyone.

The San-Phleg's greatest weaknesses are lack of motivation and discipline. He would rather socialize than work, and he tends to take life too casually. His employer often has mixed emotions—he loves San-Phleg but wishes he would be more industrious. As an executive remarked about one, "He is the nicest guy I ever fired." He rarely gets upset over anything and tends to find the bright side of everything. He is the one person most likely to tell his wife with a smile, "Look at this pink slip. I got fired today!" He usually has an endless repertoire of jokes and delights in making others laugh, often when the occasion calls for seriousness. When Jesus Christ becomes the chief object of his love, he is transformed into a more resolute, purposeful, and productive person.

The first-century evangelist Apollos is about as close as we can come to a New Testament illustration of the San-Phleg. A skilled orator who succeeded Paul and other early church founders, he did the work of stirring the churches with his Spirit-filled preaching and teaching. Loved by all, followed devotedly by some, this pleasant and dedicated man apparently traveled a great deal but did not establish new works.

## The Chlor-San

The second strongest extrovert among the blends of temperaments will be the reverse of the first—the Chlor-San. This man's life is given over completely to activity. Most of his efforts are productive and purposeful, but watch his recreation—it is so activity-prone that it borders on being violent. He is a natural pro- moter and salesman with enough charisma to get along well with others. Certainly the best moti- vator of people and one who  thrives on a challenge, he is almost fearless and exhibits boundless energy. His wife will often comment, "He has only two speeds: Wide open and stop." Chlor-San is the courtroom attorney who can charm the coldest-hearted judge and jury, the fund-raiser who can get people to con- tribute what they intended to save, the man who never goes anywhere unnoticed, the preacher who combines both practical Bible teaching and church administration, and the politician who talks his state into changing its constitution so he can represent them one more time. He is a convincing debater; what he lacks in facts or argu- ment he makes up in bluff or bravado. As a teacher, he is an excellent communicator, particularly in the social sci- ences; rarely is he drawn to math, science, or the abstract. Whatever his professional occupation, his brain is always in motion.

The weaknesses of this temperament blend, the chief of which is hostility, are as broad as his talents. He combines the quick, explosive anger of the Sanguine (without the forgiveness) and the long-burning resentment of the Cho- leric. He is the one personality type who not only gets ulcers himself, but gives them to others. Impatient with those who do not share his motivation and energy, he prides himself on being brutally frank (some call it sarcastically frank). It is difficult for him to concentrate on one thing very long, which is why he often enlists others to finish what he has started. He is opinionated, prejudiced, impetuous, and inclined doggedly to finish a project he probably should not have have started in the first place. If not controlled by God, he is apt to justify anything he does and rarely hesitates to manipulate or walk over other people to accomplish his ends. Most Chlor-Sans get so engrossed in their work that they neglect their spouses and families, even lashing out at them if they complain. The spouse of a Chlor-San becomes an emotionally shell-shocked person who feels unneeded and unloved. He or she usually admires, fears, and resents the other. When the children grow up, the spouse may leave because the Chlor-San has made him or her a nonperson. Once a Chlor-San comprehends the importance of his love and approval to his family, however, he can transform the entire household.

James, the author of the biblical book that bears his name, could well have been a Chlor-San—at least his book sounds like it. The main thrust of the book declares that "faith without works is dead!"—a favored concept by work-loving Cholerics. He used the practical and logical reasoning of a Choleric, yet was obviously a highly esteemed man of God. One human weakness he discussed—the fire of the tongue and how no man can control it (James 3)—relates directly to this temperament's most vulnerable characteristic, for we all know that Chlor-Sans feature a razor-sharp, active tongue. His victory and evident productiveness in the cause of Christ is a significant example to any thoughtful Chlor-San.

## The Chlor-Mel

The 60 percent Choleric/40 percent Melancholy is an extremely industrious and capable person. The optimism and practicality or the Choleric overcomes the tendency toward moodiness of the Melancholy, making the Chlor-Mel both goal-oriented and detailed. Possessing a quick, analytical mind, such a person usually does well in school. Being decisive, he develops into a thorough  leader, the kind whom one can always count on to do an extraordinary job. This man is the type of lawyer you would engage as a defense attorney. He is an excellent debater. In fact, never take him on in a debate unless you are assured of your facts, for he will make mincemeat of you, combining verbal aggressiveness and attendance to detail. This man is extremely competitive and forceful in all that he does. His battle plan is always the same: "Go for the jugular vein!" He is a dogged researcher and is usually successful, no matter what kind of business he pursues. The brilliant chief surgeon of a great California hospital, a Chlor-Mel, is also an extremely capable Bible teacher in his church. I know architects, plant superintendents, politicians, football coaches, preachers, businesspeople, tradespeople (though they usually end up as foremen or bosses), and leaders in many fields who are Chlor-Mels. This temperament probably makes the best natural leader. General George S. Patton, the great commander of the U.S. Third Army in World War II who drove the German forces back to Berlin, was probably a Chlor-Mel.

Equally as great as his strengths are his weaknesses. He is apt to be autocratic, a dictator-type who inspires admiration and hate simultaneously. As an opinionated person, he loves an argument, enjoys the role of devil's advocate, and will even argue against his own position just to argue. He is usually a quick-witted talker whose sarcasm can devastate others. In fact, it is not uncommon for him to keep right on jabbing, even after his victim is dead. He is a natural-born crusader whose work habits are irregular and long. Many of the leaders of activist organizations are Chlor-Mels, their philosophy of life determining which side they are on.

A Chlor-Mel harbors considerable hostility and resentment, and unless he enjoys a good love relationship with his parents, he will find interpersonal relationships difficult, particularly with his family. No one is more apt to be an overly strict disciplinarian than the Chlor-Mel parent. He or she combines the hard-to-please tendency of the Choleric and the perfectionism of the Melancholy. One such father, a supersuccessful life-insurance agent, ordered his 15-year-old son to spend all daylight hours in his room for an entire summer. Needless to say, that dad "provoked his son to wrath" and ultimately drove him away from the family and God. Chlor-Mels commonly suffer from bleeding ulcers without an organic cause, colitis, and high blood pressure; they are prime candidates for heart attacks after 50. When controlled by the Holy Spirit, however, their entire emotional life is transformed and they make outstanding Christians.

There is little doubt in my mind that the apostle Paul was a Chlor-Mel. Before his conversion he was hostile and cruel, for the Scripture teaches that he spent his time persecuting and jailing Christians. Even after his conversion, his strong-willed determination turned to unreasonable bullheadedness, as when he went up to Jerusalem against the will and warning of God. His writings and ministry demonstrate the combination of the practical-analytical reasoning and self-sacrificing but extremely driving nature of a Chlor-Mel. He is a good example of God's transforming power in the life of a Chlor-Mel who is completely dedicated to His will.

## The Chlor-Phleg

The most subdued of all the extrovertish temperaments is the Chlor-Phleg, a happy blend of the quick, active, and hot with the calm, cool, and unexcited. He is not  as apt to rush into things as quickly as other extroverts because he is more deliberate and subdued. He is extremely capable in the long run, although he does not particularly impress you that way at first. He is an organized person who combines planning activities and hard work. People usually enjoy working with and for him because he knows where he is going and has charted his course, yet he is not unduly severe with people. He has the ability to help others make the best use of their skills and rarely offends people or makes them feel used. He often gets more accomplished than any other temperament because he has no inclination to do it all himself and invariably thinks in terms of enlisting others in his work. His motto reads "Why do the work of ten people when you can get ten people to do the work?"

A Chlor-Phleg minister who organized one of my Family Life Seminars recently exemplified this temperament when it became necessary because of a larger attendance than we had expected to move hundreds of books to another place. Instead of furiously carrying them all downstairs himself, he looked the crowd over and quietly collected ten people to help him. The whole process took four minutes and he carried only one load of books. The Chlor-Phleg's slogan on organization states "Anything that needs to be done can be done better if it's organized." These people are usually good husbands or wives and fathers or mothers as well as excellent administrators in almost any field.

In spite of his obvious capabilities, the Chlor-Phleg is not without a notable set of weaknesses. Although not as addicted to the quick anger of some temperaments, he is known to harbor resentment and bitterness. Some of the cutting edge of the Choleric's sarcasm is offset by the gracious spirit of the Phlegmatic, so instead of uttering cutting and cruel remarks, his barbs are more apt to emerge as cleverly disguised humor. One is never quite sure whether he is kidding or ridiculing, depending on his mood. No one can be more bullheadedly stubborn than a Chlor-Phleg, and it is difficult for him to change his mind once it is committed. Repentance or the acknowledgment of a mistake is not at all easy for him. Consequently, he will be more apt to make it up to those he has wronged without really facing his mistake. The worrisome traits of the Phlegmatic side of his nature may so curtail his adventurous tendencies that he never quite measures up to his capabilities.

Titus, the spiritual son of the apostle Paul and leader of the hundred or so churches on the Isle of Crete, may well have been a Chlor-Phleg. When filled with the Spirit, he was the kind of man on whom Paul could depend to faithfully teach the Word to the churches and administrate them capably for the glory of God. The book Paul wrote to him makes ideal reading for any teacher, particularly a Chlor-Phleg.

## The Mel-San

Now we turn to the predominantly introvertish temperaments. Each will look somewhat similar to one we have already examined, except that the two temperaments will be reversed in intensity. Such variation accounts for the exciting individuality in human beings. Mel-San is usually a gifted person, fully capable of being a performing arts musician who can steal the heart of an audience. As an artist, he not only draws or paints beautifully but can also sell his own work—if he's in the right mood. Industry uses such a man in production control and cost analysis; often he can work his way up to a supervisory position. It is not uncommon to encounter him in the field of education, for he makes a good scholar and probably the best of all classroom teachers, particularly on the high school and college levels. The Melancholy in him will ferret out little-known facts and be exacting in the use of events and detail, while the Sanguine 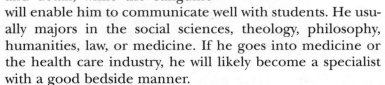 will enable him to communicate well with students. He usually majors in the social sciences, theology, philosophy, humanities, law, or medicine. If he goes into medicine or the health care industry, he will likely become a specialist with a good bedside manner.

Sometimes the Mel-San will go into sales, but it will usually be low-pressure selling that calls for exacting detail and the presentation of many facts, as in computers, calculators, cash registers, textbooks, and so on. He also makes a good lawyer, dentist, or doctor. In fact, almost anything in the medical field is open to hin. It may come as a surprise to you, but many great actors, opera stars, and country-western singers are Mel-Sans. Give one a guitar and he can usually delight an audience for hours. He is a delightful emcee, and if he enters into the ministry, he will become a good preacher because he will study thoroughly to offer a substantive message in an interesting style. As a minister, he usually wears well with his people. Almost any craft or trade welcomes him. A Mel-San is often a loyal spouse and devoted parent if he or she learns to accept people and not be too critical of them. Although extremely capable, the Mel-San usually works for someone else and rarely is venturesome enough to launch out in his own business or found an organization.

Mel-Sans show an interesting combination of mood swings. Be sure of this: Mel-San is an emotional creature! When circumstances are pleasing to him, he can reflect a fantastically happy mood. But if things work out badly or he is rejected, insulted, or injured, he drops into such a mood that his lesser Sanguine nature drowns in the resultant sea of self-pity. Like any predominant Melancholy, he must guard his thinking process or he will destroy himself. He is easily moved to tears and feels everything deeply, but he can be unreasonably critical and hard on others. He tends to be rigid and usually will not cooperate unless things go his way, which is often idealistic and impractical. As a college student he gets superior grades but may take five or six years to finish because he changes his major so many times. It is not unlike him to abandon his education, which makes it difficult for him to measure up to his potential. He is often a fearful, insecure person with a poor self-image that limits him unnecessarily. These people are much more capable than they realize, but they internalize so much that others often do not recognize their potential. This temperament blend is responsible for most of the folk tunes and ballads of our day. Listen carefully and you will often detect a melancholic lament, mournful wail, or ballad of doom by the singer. If he has undergone a tragic experience or been rejected in love, watch out! Before he finishes, the tune will lower your mood to match his. As a counselor with a yen to help Melancholies experience upbeat emotions a majority of the time, I know what the power of God can do for them if they learn the habit of thanksgiving thinking (1 Thessalonians 5:18); it can transform their lives.

Many of the prophets were Mel-Sans—John the Baptist, Elijah, Jeremiah, and others. They had a tremendous capacity to commune with God; they were self-sacrificing people—helpers who had enough charisma to attract a following; they tended to be legalistic in their teachings and calls to repentance; they exhibited a flair of the dramatic; and they willingly died for their principles. Even some of these godly men had problems with depression.

## The Mel-Chlor

The mood swings of the Melancholy are usually stabilized by the Mel-Chlor's self-will and determination. There is almost nothing vocationally that this person cannot do well. He is both a perfectionist and a driver. He makes an excellent attorney, particularly in fields that demand research and accuracy, such as corporate law, securities, or taxes. And because he prepares twice as hard for a case  as anyone else, he seldom loses. As a doctor, he is familiar with the last word in medicine—and usually lets you know that he knows. He possesses strong leadership capabilities, enjoys being chairman of the board, and never comes to a meeting unprepared. He is more apt to be a family dentist than a specialist, but may give up dentistry after 15 to 20 years to go into something else. I have noticed that many airline captains are Mel-Chlors, mixing precision with decisiveness and determination. As an educator, he often leaves the classroom for administration. He could become an executive vice president of practically any well-organized business and improve it. Almost any craft, construction, or educational level is open to him. Unlike the Mel-San, he may found his own institution or business and run it capably—not with noise and color but with efficiency. Many a great orchestra leader and choral conductor is a Mel-Chlor. He often goes into politics, as evidenced by the fact that many of our founding fathers could well have been Mel-Chlors, and a variety of athletic fields attract him. Many superstars (particularly baseball pitchers), some above-average quarterbacks, and a number of running backs are of this mixture of temperaments. Numerous mission boards, colleges, and Christian organizations were founded by Spirit-dedicated Mel-Chlors.

The natural weaknesses of Mel-Chlors reveal themselves in the mind, emotions, and mouth. They are extremely difficult people to please, rarely satisfying even themselves. Once they start thinking negatively about something or someone (including themselves), they can be intolerable to live with. Their mood follows their thought process. Although they do not retain a depressed mood as long as the other two blends of the Melancholy, they can lapse into it more quickly.

The two basic temperaments haunted by self-persecution, hostility, and criticism are the Melancholy and the Choleric. Put those together in a Mel-Chlor and look for him under the pile as soon as things go wrong. His favorite prayer is "Lord, why me?" It is not uncommon for him to get angry at God as well as his fellowman, and if such thoughts persist long enough, he may become manic-depressive. In extreme cases, he can become sadistic. When confronted with his vile thinking pattern and angry, bitter spirit, he can be expected to explode.

His penchant for detailed analysis and perfection tends to make him a nitpicker who drives others up the wall. Unless he is filled with God's Spirit or can maintain a positive frame of mind, he is not enjoyable company for long periods of time. No one is more painfully aware of this, of course, than his spouse and children. He not only emotes disapproval, but he also feels compelled to castigate them verbally for their failures and to correct their mistakes—in public as well as in private. He usually strips his spouse of all psychological self-protection by his spirit and words of condemnation and criticism until she feels dehumanized. Unless his children are perfectionists, he treats them the same way. He finds it difficult to be aroused sexually when in bed with his wife unless her housekeeping has passed his "white-glove inspection." A Mel-Chlor has been known to withhold sex from his wife for months because she didn't please him in the way she cooked, cleaned house, or handled the money. His attitude is "That should teach her." This person, by nature, desperately needs the love of God in his heart, and his family needs him to share it with them.

Many of the great men of the Bible show signs of a Mel-Chlor temperament. Two that come to mind are 1) Paul's tireless traveling companion, Dr. Luke, the painstaking scholar who carefully researched the life of Christ and left the church the most detailed account of our Lord's life, as well as the only record of the spread of the early church, and 2) Moses, the great leader of Israel. Like many Mel–Chlors, the latter never gained victory over his hostility and bitterness. Consequently, he died before his time. Like Moses, who wasted 40 years on the back side of the desert harboring bitterness and animosity before surrendering his life to God, many a Mel-Chlor never lives up to his amazing potential because of the spirit of anger and revenge. Learning to "walk in the Spirit" and not in his Mel-Chlor flesh can literally transform his life.

## The Mel-Phleg

The greatest scholars the world has ever known have been Mel-Phlegs. They are not nearly as prone to hostility as the two previous Melancholies and usually get along well with others. These gifted introverts combine the analytical perfectionism of the Melancholy with the organized efficiency of the Phlegmatic. They are usually good-natured humanitarians who prefer a quiet solitary environment for study and research to the

endless round of activities sought by the more extrovertish temperaments. Mel-Phlegs are usually excellent spellers and good mathematicians. In addition to higher education, they excel in medicine, pharmacy, dentistry, architecture, decorating, literature, theology, and many other cerebral fields. They are highly respected writers, philosophers, and scientists, masters in the crafts, construction, music, and art. Extremely detail conscious and accurate, they make good accountants and bookkeepers. If they enter medicine or dentistry, it is not uncommon for them to become specialists.

During the past few years, my family dentist has sent me several times to a dental clinic for root-canal work. All these dentists are specialists and, interestingly enough, all are Mel-Phlegs. These gifted people have greatly benefited humanity. Most of the world's significant inventions and medical discoveries have been made by Mel-Phlegs. One such individual whom I know well is so gifted that I have said, "He is the only man I know who is incapable of incompetence."

Despite his abilities, the Mel-Phleg, like the rest of us, has his own potential weaknesses. Unless controlled by God, he easily becomes discouraged and develops a negative thinking pattern. But once he realizes it is a sin to develop the spirit of criticism and learns to rejoice evermore, his entire outlook on life can be transformed. Ordinarily a quiet person, he is capable of inner angers and hostility caused by his tendency to be revengeful. If he indulges it long enough, he can even be vindictive.

I know two brilliant Mel-Phlegs with a number of similarities. Both are the best in their fields, highly competent, and well paid. Both are family men and active Christians, but there the comparison ends. One is loved and admired by his family and many friends. He is a self-taught Bible scholar and one of the greatest men I know. The other man is antisocial, not respected by his family, disliked by others, and miserable. The difference? The second man became bitter years ago, and today it influences his entire life, in fact, it even shows on his face.

Mel-Phlegs are unusually vulnerable to fear, anxiety, and a negative self-image. It has always amazed me that the people with the greatest talents and capabilities are often victimized by genuine feelings of poor self-worth.

In addition to enduring mood swings, they are so stubborn and rigid that they too easily become implacable and uncooperative. Their strong tendency to be conscientious allows them to let others pressure them into making commitments that drain their energy and creativity. When filled with God's Spirit, these people are loved and admired by their families because their personal self-discipline and dedication are exemplary in the home, even though humanitarian concerns may cause them to neglect their families. Unless they learn to pace themselves and enjoy diversions that help them relax, they often become early mortality statistics.

The most likely Mel-Phleg in the Bible is the beloved apostle John. He obviously had a sensitive nature, for as a youth he laid his head on Jesus' breast at the Lord's Supper. On one occasion he became so angry at some people that he asked the Lord Jesus to call fire from heaven down on them. Yet at the crucifixion he was the lone disciple who devotedly stood at the cross. As Jesus died, John was the one to whom he entrusted his mother. Later the disciple became a great church leader and left us five books in the New Testament, two of which, the Gospel of John and the book of Revelation, particularly glorify Jesus Christ.

## The Phleg-San

The easiest of the 12 temperament blends to get along with over a protracted period of time is the Phleg-San. He is congenial, happy, cooperative, thoughtful, people-oriented, diplomatic, dependable, fun loving, and humorous. A favorite with children and adults, he never displays an abrasive personality. Rarely does he take up a career in sales, although he could do it well if he represented a good firm where high-pressure selling was not required. He is often found in education and also makes an excellent administrator, college registrar, accountant, mechanic, funeral director, working scientist, engineer, statistician, radio announcer, counselor, visitation minister, veterinarian, farmer, bricklayer, or construction worker. He is usually a good family man who enjoys a quiet life and loves his wife and children. Ordinarily he deports himself honorably and becomes a favorite in the neighborhood. If he is a Christian and attends a church where the pastor is a good motivator, he probably takes an active role in the church.

The weaknesses of a Phleg-San are as gentle as his personality—unless you have to live with him all the time. Since he inherited the lack of motivation of a Phlegmatic and the lack of discipline of a Sanguine, it is not uncommon for the Phleg-San to fall far short of his true capabilities. He often quits school, passes up good opportunities, and avoids anything that involves "too much effort." He tends to putter around, enjoys solitude, and doesn't seem to mind that the years pass him by and he doesn't go anywhere. Since opposites tend to attract each other in marriage, a Phleg-San woman will often marry an aggressive man who carries her through life. When the man is a Phleg-San, it's a different ball game. A wife finds it difficult to carry her husband vocationally, and his passive ways often become a source of irritation to her. The Phleg-San's wife buys him every new self-improvement book that hits the market, but he falls asleep reading them. The most common question I am asked at my Family Life Seminars is

"How does a Choleric wife motivate a Phlegmatic husband?" One Choleric woman's answer was, "When you get him up, keep him moving."

Fear is another problem that accentuates his unrealistic feelings of insecurity. With just 10 percent more faith he could be transformed from his timidity and self-defeating anxieties, but he prefers to build a self-protective shell around himself and selfishly avoid the kind of involvement or commitment to activity that he needs and that would be a rich blessing to his partner and children. I have tremendous respect for the potential of these happy, contented people, but they must cooperate by letting God motivate them to unselfish activity.

The man in the Scripture who reminds me most of the Phleg-San is gentle, faithful, good-natured Timothy, the favorite spiritual son of the apostle Paul. He was dependable and steady but timid and fearful. Repeatedly, Paul had to urge him to be more aggressive and to "do the work of an evangelist" (2 Timothy 4:5).

## The Phleg-Chlor

The most active of all Phlegmatics is the Phleg-Chlor, but it must be remembered that since he is predominantly a Phlegmatic, he will never be a ball of fire. Like his brother Phlegmatics, he is easy to get along with and may become an excellent group leader, foreman, executive vice-president, accountant, educator, planner, and laborer in almost any area of construction. The Phlegmatic has the potential to become a good counselor, for he is an excellent listener, does not interrupt the client with stories about himself, and is genuinely interested in other people. Although the Phleg-Chlor rarely

offers his services to others, when they come to his organized office where he exercises control, he is professional. His advice will be practical, helpful, and if he is a
Bible-taught Christian, quite trustworthy. He has the
patience of Job and often is able to help those who have
not found relief with other counselors. His gentle spirit
never makes people feel threatened. He always does the
right thing, but rarely goes beyond the norm. If his wife
can make the adjustment to his passive lifestyle and
reluctance to take the lead in the home, particularly in
the discipline of their children, they can enjoy a happy
marriage.

The weaknesses of the Phleg-Chlor are not readily
apparent but gradually come to the surface, especially in
the home. In addition to the lack of motivation and the
fear problems of the other Phlegmatics, he can be determinedly stubborn and unyielding. He doesn't blow up at
others but simply refuses to give in or cooperate. He is
not a fighter by nature but often lets his inner anger and
stubbornness reflect itself in silence. One such man with
a fast-talking wife said, "I've finally learned how to handle
that woman!" When I asked, "How?" he replied, "Silence!
Last week I didn't talk to her for five days—she can't
stand it!" I warned him that he had chosen the well-paved
boulevard to ulcers. Little did I realize what a prophet I
was, for he was rushed to the hospital 28 days later with
bleeding ulcers.

The Phleg-Chlor often retreats to his workshop alone
or nightly immerses his mind in TV. The older he gets, the
more he selfishly indulges his sedentary tendency and
becomes increasingly passive. Although he will probably
live a long and peaceful life, if he indulges these passive
feelings, it is a boring life—not only for him but also for his
family. He needs to give himself to the concerns and needs
of his family. This is one of the few types that should take

on more than they think they can do, for they work well under pressure and are externally motivated.

No man in the Bible epitomizes the Phleg-Chlor better than Abraham in the Old Testament. Fear characterized everything he did in the early days. For instance, he was reluctant to leave the security of the pagan city of Ur when God first called him; he even denied his wife on two occasions and tried to palm her off as his sister because of fear. Finally, he surrendered completely to God and grew in his Spirit. Accordingly, his greatest weakness became his greatest strength. Today, instead of being known as fearful Abraham, he has the reputation of being "the man who believed God and it was counted unto him for righteousness."

### The Phleg-Mel

Of all the temperament blends, the Phleg-Mel is the most gracious, gentle, and quiet. He is rarely angry or hostile and almost never says anything for which he must apologize (mainly because he rarely says much). He never embarrasses himself or others, always does the proper thing, dresses simply, is dependable and exact. He tends to exhibit the natural gifts of mercy and help, and he is neat and organized in his working habits. He does well in photography, printing, inventory, analysis, layout, advertising, mechanics, education, pharmacy, dentistry, finish carpentry (almost never piecework or production—he is a plodder), glassblowing, wallpaper hanging, painting, or anything that involves intricate detail and great patience. Like any Phlegmatic, he is handy around the house and as energy permits will keep his home in good repair. If he has a wife who recognizes his tendencies toward passivity (but tactfully waits for him to take the lead in the home and for biblical reasons labors at submission), they will have a good family life and marriage. If she resents his reticence to lead and be aggressive, however, she may become discontented and foment marital strife. Unless taught properly in his church, he may neglect the discipline necessary to help prepare his children for a productive, self-disciplined life. Although he seldom admits it, a passive father who lets his children grow up sassing and disobeying him and their mother is just as guilty of "provoking his children to wrath" as the angry tyrant whose unreasonable discipline makes them bitter.

The other weaknesses of this man revolve around fear, selfishness, negativism, criticism, and lack of self-image. Recently a good-looking young painter acknowledged at one of our Family Life Seminars that my wife's talk on fear really spoke to him, and for the first time he was willing to face the fact that fear was a sin. Her presentation made him acutely aware of his reluctance to take advantage of a tremendous business opportunity that confronted him. As he talked, I could tell that here was a superbly qualified and dedicated Phleg-Mel who had been selling himself short. Someone has said, "There are two kinds of thinkers—those who think they can and those who think they can't—and they are both right." Once a Phleg-Mel realizes that only his fears and negative feelings about himself keep him from succeeding, he is able to come out of his shell and become an effective man, husband, and father. Most Phleg-Mels have an obsession against involvement. They are so afraid of overextending themselves or getting overinvolved that they automatically refuse almost any kind of affiliation. I have never seen a Phleg-Mel overinvolved in anything—except in keeping from getting overinvolved. He must recognize that since he is not internally motivated, he definitely needs to accept more responsibility than he thinks he can fulfill, for that external stimulation will motivate him to greater achievement. All Phlegmatics work well under pressure, but it must come from outside. In addition to cultivating his spiritual life, a Phleg-Mel should give special thought to taking vitamins and keeping his body toned through physical exercise, which can give him a whole new lease on life. His greatest source of motivation, of course, will be the power of the Holy Spirit.

Barnabas, the godly saint of the first-century church who accompanied the apostle Paul on his first missionary journey, was in all probability a Phleg-Mel. He was the man who gave half his goods to the early church to feed the poor, the man who contended with Paul over providing John Mark, his nephew, with another chance to serve God by accompanying them on the second missionary journey. Although the contention became so sharp that Barnabas took his nephew and they proceeded on their journey alone, Paul later commended Mark, saying, "for he is profitable to me for the ministry" (2 Timothy 4:11 KJV). Today we have the Gospel of Mark because faithful, dedicated, and gentle Barnabas was willing to help him over a hard place in his life. Phleg-Mels respond to the needs of others if they will just let themselves move out into the stream of life and work with people where they are.

• • •

At the risk of making the natural attraction of temperaments more complicated than necessary, I deem it essential to point out that it is an oversimplification to maintain that Sanguines attract Melancholies and Cholerics attract Phlegmatics (and vice versa). Further research leads me to believe that more often than not we are attracted to the temperament combination that most complements our own. While many exceptions arise because there is often a fine line between the three combination blends of each of the four temperaments, we will often find the following combinations getting together.

## San-Chlors Attract Mel-Phlegs

As a general rule, the strongest of the extrovert combinations, the San-Chlor, is attracted to the Mel-Phleg. This unites the fun-loving, activist driver with the deep-thinking, easygoing individual. Emotionally, the most hot-tempered, explosive type of person often marries a deep-feeling, fear-prone individual. You can just imagine how the articulate sarcasm of the angry extrovert, who often says whatever comes into his mind, can crush the spirit of the easily offended Mel-Phleg who brings a lack of self-image into their marriage.

## San-Mels Attract Mel-Sans

It is not uncommon to find the most emotionally expressive temperament, the San-Mel combination, marrying a Mel-San. Both are extremely emotional and caring people by nature. One loves to make others happy; the other likes to be made happy. Hopefully, their broad mood swings from ecstasy to depression will not occur on the same day, so they can be an uplifting influence on their partner. These blends coming together in marriage allow them to understand each other and accept each other's mood swings. Both are verbal people, the San-Mel speaking his mind at will, whether it offends his partner or not. The Mel-San remembers every mistake, offense, or thoughtless deed of her partner, and both are never far from tears. Mel-Sans can cry at the drop of a hat; in fact, tears are their first emotional response to anything sad or disappointing—including misplaced laundry tickets, forgotten telephone numbers, and impertinent sales ladies. A day for them is not complete until they have had a good cry.

## San-Phlegs Attract Mel-Chlors

This combination brings the most lovable and possibly most easy-to-like personality together with the most serious-minded of all temperaments. The fun-loving San-Phleg doesn't care if school keeps or not just so he has a good time. The other measures the success of his day by the amount of work completed. These two types will endlessly grate on each other unless they learn the art of adjustment. San-Phlegs, who love praise and approval, will instead receive criticism and condemnation from their Mel-Chlor mates. I have watched San-Phleg women lose their outgoing, happy charm under the continual blast of their Mel-Chlor mate's disapproval. San-Phleg men tend to respond to withering criticism by having an affair—sometimes just to hurt their partner.

## Chlor-Sans Attract Phleg-Mels

The hard driving and persuasive Chlor-San usually marries the super introvert Phleg-Mel. The Chlor-San, whether male or female, will be the automatic leader of the family, which may produce silent resentment in the partner. A Phleg-Mel is often much more capable than he realizes. Therefore, if he lets his activist-oriented mate motivate him, he will accomplish much more than he would alone. But if he becomes resentful of his partner's prodding, he will dig in his heels and refuse to budge. It's the old case of "the irresistible force meeting the immovable object."

## Chlor-Mels Attract Phleg-Sans

Chlor-Mels are the ultimate workaholics. Goal-oriented, motivated, and detailed, they are decisive, forceful, takeover types and among the most verbally critical. The Phleg-San partner, however, is often the easiest of all temperaments to get along with. He is a congenial, fun-loving, humorous, natural-born peacemaker. Talk about contrast! The one most likely to pick a fight often marries the type who would much rather make peace than war. The success of their marriage will usually be determined by whether the diplomacy of the one modulates the domineering tendencies of the other.

## Chlor-Phlegs Attract Phleg-Chlors

The most subdued of all the extroverts, the deliberate activist Chlor-Phleg, who is well-organized and the most gracious of the three Choleric styles, is a good match for the Phleg-Chlor, who possesses some of the same latent tendencies but often waits until prodded before setting out to accomplish anything. These two, if resentment and stubborn resistance do not predominate, can effect a full and meaningful relationship.

## No Wrong Temperament Combinations

Don't be surprised if you and your partner are not one of the ideal combinations listed above. Actually, only four of the possible 12 are perfect opposites: San-Mel/Mel-San or the reverse; Chlor-Phleg/Phleg-Chlor or the reverse. All the other predominant temperaments are opposites but their secondary temperaments may be similar. Besides, you may not fall into any of these categories, for a San-Chlor may marry a Chlor-Mel or some other combination. I am not contending that the above six combinations are exclusive but that they tend to predominate. In fact, as I have already acknowledged, my wife and I are a Chlor-San/Phleg-San combination, and as such we do not fit the mold presented above.

Ordinarily, the two primary temperaments are the ones that count. They will usually be opposites, but even that is not always true, for, as you know, temperament attraction is not the only motivation for marriage. For instance, those who are eager to flee an unhappy home life may catch the first freight train to come along. Just this week a 50-year-old woman admitted that she married at 15 because she wanted desperately to escape from her father, who had been molesting her since she was 12. Unfortunately, in her haste she married a man similar to her father and spent the next 15 years in a living nightmare.

I am very anxious that you do not miss my point here: While certain opposite temperament combinations attract each other in marriage as a general rule, that neither mandates a happy adjustment nor guarantees a life of harmony. For . . .

## Other Factors Are Also Involved

So far I have said very little about the other factors which help to make up your behavior. Temperament is a powerful influence on behavior, but it is only one such influence. Your background, childhood, and education also exercise a powerful influence on you, as do your religious and moral convictions, together with the powerful force of self-discipline (or lack of it). Thus is why two people of identical temperament combinations can manifest different behaviors. The diagram on the next page illustrates to some degree those differing influences.

We have already noted the powerful influence of temperament on our behavior, estimated somewhere between 20 and 35 percent. The second dominant area is identified by psychologists as the environmental factors, including childhood training, the love or lack of love received in childhood, traumatizing experiences (divorce, injury, frequent moves during adolescence, etc.), education, etc. The third very significant force in human behavior is a person's religious-moral commitment. Humanistic psychology has little room for this factor in human behavior, which only reveals the intellectual poverty of that so-called "science." I have found that religious convictions can actually be awesome in their influence on a person's life, and provide the only power I know for meaningful change.

# Behavior Formula

Inherited temperament
Childhood training
Life's experiences
Mental attitude
Self-discipline
Parental love
Motivation
Education
Health
+      Habit

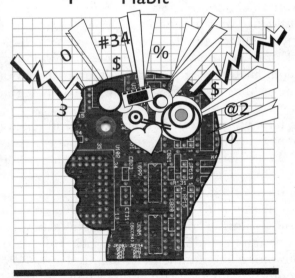

# = Your Behavior

Diagram 1: Behavior Formula

Let me illustrate. Two people of identical temperament combinations with similar environmental backgrounds can be moving along on opposite paths, based on their religious values. Take, for example, a committed Christian of noble character who is committed to fidelity, truth, honor, and the other moral values taught in Scripture. Now compare him to a product of a secular humanist education, which dominates most public schools today from kindergarten through college. The self-centered or "self-actualized autonomy" taught for those 17 or more years will usually produce a moral relativist—that is, a person who rejects moral absolutes and insists that anything which seems right is permissible. Such a person will have a much higher selfishness quotient than one who has been taught exclusively the Christian moral ethic of love—giving and serving.

For this reason it is always best for Christians to seek Christian companions, and moral relativists to court those who share their amoral tastes. Asking a moral relativist to commit himself to loving, honoring, and providing sexual exclusivity "for as long as you both shall live" is a cruel hoax, especially in today's culture among those who have adopted the humanistic, no-values lifestyle. As Dr. Alan Bloom pointed out in his bestselling book, *The Closing of the American Mind,* relativism has produced the idea that morality, decency, commitment, and honor are "no big deal." A pastor friend told of a college girl who grew up in his church, "as pretty as a girl can get in 21 years." Her question startled him into a new awareness of the younger generation's moral perspective. "Pastor, I need your advice. How can I get the man I'm living with to marry me?" When he asked her what virginity meant to her, she replied, "Being a virgin today is no big deal!"

Where did that young woman gain those values? Certainly not in Sunday school, church, or her Christian home.

It was the direct result of a humanistic education in our secular public schools, which we Christians help to support through our taxes. This is just one of the many reasons today for sending children to a Christian school or home schooling them.

Two identical temperaments with similar environments will live differently on the basis of one force alone. One's attitude toward virtue will significantly affect marriage adjustment if the couple shares the same moral-spiritual convictions and experiences. Two people with similar religious commitment should have a much easier time adjusting than those who have none.

Now look back at our diagram on page 92. Another important factor must be considered: the ever-present force of self-discipline. As most athletic coaches, music teachers, and other instructors will agree, "Discipline is the name of the game." It is often even more important than talent. A gifted individual in any field is destined for eventual failure unless he develops self-discipline, and that is particularly true of interpersonal adjustment.

Spouse-abusers are not always Choleric-Melancholy temperaments—that is, the most explosive and angry of all temperaments. Many Chlor-Mels have never struck another person in anger, nor have many Chlor-Sans, the second-most-explosive temperament. Why? They are too self-disciplined, and such an action would violate their moral-spiritual convictions. We need to understand that spouse abuse is the epitome of undisciplined selfishness. It seems to be an expanding phenomenon in our society today because humanism teaches us, "Do your own thing," "Be your own person," and "You owe it to yourself."

Discipline takes self-denial and requires self-control; it includes follow-through and consistency. Such traits are not found in all the temperaments, nor do they always appear in one's childhood training, but they are the product of the Holy Spirit's ministry in the life of the Christian. Galatians

5:22,23 tells us that one of "the fruit [or results] of the Spirit is ... self-control." As I have made clear in all my other books on temperament, the individual who truly wants to strengthen his weaknesses will submit to the ministry of the Spirit-controlled life.

## Any Two Can Adjust

Married couples often ask, "What is the ideal temperament combination for marriage?" My answer always is the same: "Whatever temperaments the two of you have!" There are no two perfect temperament combinations, for all have both strengths and weaknesses (about 15 of each). And since we all contain at least two temperaments, a primary and a secondary, then we all have, to one degree or another, as many as 30 strengths and 30 weaknesses. If we add to that the other influences on a person's temperament, you can readily see that it is impossible to pick the ideal temperament combination. The Creator has selected each of our temperaments for His own good pleasure. We need only make it acceptable to Him. When couples are having trouble, they are prone to think that their conflicting temperament combinations have become the problem, but that is only a symptom of a much deeper issue, which we shall address in the next section of this book.

Two very wounded Christian workers were referred to me by their pastor, who fretted, "I have come to the end of my rope." He was a Chlor-Mel, she a Mel-Chlor, but they thought they represented identical temperaments. That is not unusual, either because the individuals don't fully understand the temperaments or because they don't completely know themselves. Because both were articulate and very critical, they were destroying each other with their mouths. Even though Cholerics are more verbal than Melancholies, women tend to be more verbal than men, so both were used to speaking their minds. Filled with the spirit of criticism, they were annihilating each other with their tongues. Understanding the temperaments helped those two only marginally, for they needed to recognize their personal sin instead of being so occupied with their partner's sin. I will save for a later illustration the advice I gave, but I am happy to say that they are lovers today and are still actively engaged in the Lord's work.

This only underscores the good news that any two temperaments can make a happy adjustment—*if* they want to.

# 9

## OPPOSITES
### *Attract*

# *Strengthening Your Temperament Weaknesses*

Only one source of power can so significantly modify our behavior that we will appear to change our temperament. As already stated, temperament is a permanent part of our lives—just like physical appearance, which can be modified to some degree but never really changes. As the Bible says, we are all "fearfully and wonderfully made." If you were born to be five feet eleven inches in height, that will not vary much during your lifetime. If you were born a Chlor-Mel, you will live and die a Chlor-Mel.

I can just hear you say, "But I know people who have changed!" I hear this statement all the time, but people fail to realize that they are simply observing *the strengthening of a person's weakness,* which seems to reflect a change. Suppose a Phleg-San is raised in an austere and overstrict family. His introvertish temperament, combined with a strong tendency toward fear, will cause him to grow up as an extremely reserved and fearful person. Later in life, with the power of God and the right kind of encouragement from his married partner, he will come out of his shell and become much more outgoing. But the temperament combination did not change. The Holy Spirit strengthened the weaknesses of fear and self-protection, giving the appearance of change.

God has granted to every person certain talents and strengths at conception. This would include his temperament, IQ, body type, appearance, and other characteristics. Since we are all members of the Adamic race, it follows that because of the fall we also inherit deficiencies, often labeled temperament weaknesses: birth defects, predispositions, etc. The whole person, of course, is not just temperament or physical makeup, but both of these, together with the other influences already examined—including the will, self-discipline, and religious or spiritual commitment—create the composite person, a unique blend of strengths and weaknesses.

Nothing has a more powerful influence on a misshapen temperament, subject to negative behavior, than a genuine conversion experience, for that introduces the power of God into a person's life. You may protest, "But I know Christians who are not changed." I do too. But that is not God's fault. They were given sufficient power from above to effect meaningful change in their behavior, but they failed to use that power. As a result, they may experience a lifetime of anxiety and distress, or even tragedy.

One of the biggest misconceptions in the Christian world is that the changed life of the believer is automatic—as though a person who "called upon the name of the Lord" would instantaneously undergo a metamorphosis. When we sincerely call on the name of the Lord Jesus Christ, He comes into our life, cleanses us from all sin, and provides us the potential for change—but only the potential. From then on we must pursue a lifetime of cooperation with the Holy Spirit, who resides within us to fulfill God's revolutionary blueprint.

Have you ever considered the abundant provisions which God has afforded every believer? First we receive salvation and cleansing; then we are indwelt by the Spirit of

God, who "abides with us forever." In addition, God has given us His Word, which can have a powerful effect on our spiritual life *if* we use it. The Bible is likened to food: It does us no good unless we ingest it. The Christian who regularly takes time to read, hear, study, memorize, and meditate on the Word of God will "be strong in the Lord and in the power of his might." The Christian who neglects God's Word will be weak—so weak that his change of behavior will be minimal, and so minimal that many people will wonder whether he ever became a Christian.

God has given us the potential for change through the indwelling Holy Spirit, the Bible, the church (which should be an indispensable part of a Christian's life), Christian fellowship, books like this, tapes, and so on. But just as all people are born physical babies, so all Christians are born again as spiritual babies, requiring the milk of the Word to grow strong in the Lord. First John 2:12-14 introduces three stages of spiritual growth which are identical to the three stages of physical growth: children, young people, and fathers. (Study that passage carefully.)

But just as surely as physical babies will never develop unless fed properly, so it is with spiritual infants. Therefore many Christians we have met through the years have never grown up. The potential for spiritual growth and for temperamental maturity has been present all the time, but they did not avail themselves of it. Only when we use the resources of God will we become strong enough to effect temperament change.

If we expect God to do it all for us as a free gift, similar to His gift of salvation, forget it. He imparted salvation freely because there was no possible way for us to save ourselves or even contribute the tiniest measure of grace to our salvation. He did it all! But as we begin to make our way down the path of spiritual maturity, He expects us to do our part. Just as a baby must suck milk into his body and eventually eat the bread and meat which God has provided, we need to feed on the Word of God to mature spiritually. We are saved freely by simply receiving God's gift of eternal life, "calling on the name of the Lord," but growth "in grace and knowledge of the Lord" depends on our consistent effort. God has given us the potential for change; now we must freely exercise our free will in response to that provision.

## My Counseling Secret Revealed

I have never told this story before, but I consider this an appropriate place to insert it as an illustration. During the 40 years I was a pastor, I spent a considerable amount of time counseling. I enjoy preaching to crowds, but I also relish helping people one-on-one as individuals. Most of my graduate training, including my doctorate from Western Baptist Seminary, centered upon counseling, and I have studied almost every major technique imaginable, from Freud to Rogers to reality therapy. Dr. Henry Brandt, one of the first Christian psychologists who tested all systems of counseling against the Scriptures for validity, helped me develop my own biblical style. It must have been effective, for though I have never advertised or purposely tried to promote myself as a counselor, more than 6000 people have found their way to my office or home. Quite often one troubled person has referred his disturbed friends to me for counseling. Admittedly, I didn't help everyone who came to me; no counselor does, for it takes the counselee's cooperation to produce meaningful change.

I entered counseling at a time when it was fashionable for people in distress to seek a counselor for therapy every week for as long as nine months, then twice a month for one year, then once a month for at least another year. At 75 dollars an interview, a counselor made a comfortable living. As a pastor, I did not charge for my counseling service because the church I served paid me a salary. That was sometimes a source of irritation, for I recognized that people seldom value anything they receive for free.

Then one day the Lord gave me an incredible idea that revolutionized my success rate. I began to charge counselees—not money, but *time!* I explained that the first interview was free of charge, but from then on they were obliged to spend at least 20 minutes a day keeping the spiritual prescription that I had written out for them, or I would refuse to see them again. Like a medical doctor who dispensed a prescription and expected the patient to take it faithfully between office calls, I knew that if they attended to my spiritual prescription at least five days a week, they would get better.

The prescription, which was very simple, started with church attendance. If they came to church once a week, I had them increase to twice a week, convinced that hearing the Bible taught is profitable for everyone. Then I prescribed that they read a four-chapter Bible passage daily and keep a spiritual diary (as outlined in my book *How to Study the Bible for Yourself*). Next came one verse of Scripture a week to be memorized, and one of my books to read (usually a temperament book or one that focused upon the problem they were facing). Finally I gave them a simple formula for regular daily prayer.

Any experienced pastor will recognize what I was doing—discipling my counselees. Each week we talked about their problems and considered all questions related to their assignment, but I also checked up on their prescription progress and added another for the next week. I was not surprised to find that counselees did not become counseling-dependent; instead, their overall spiritual health improved. I never saw an individual more than seven times, for by that time (or sooner) he was well enough to stand on his own two feet and continue growing in the Word of God, either by attending a small-group Bible study or developing a personal study.

Frankly, most believers do not need a counselor to grow in Christ. They can do it on their own, and most Christians do.

All of God's people face problems, some of them serious enough to demand the attention of a counselor, but most Christians go promptly to the Word of God for direction and are sustained and strengthened by the indwelling Holy Spirit. Gradually God will change them and give them power to cope with their situation.

One of the best-kept secrets in Christianity today is the tangible dynamic of God to alter the lives of people after their conversion. Very honestly, I have never seen a mis-shapen temperament combination that God's power cannot modify—*if* the individual is willing to be changed. And that potential for change is guaranteed by . . .

## The Power of the Cross

> The message of the cross is foolishness to those who are perishing, but to us who are being saved it is the power of God (1 Corinthians 1:18).

Next to John 3:16, the above verse is one of the most important proclamations in Scripture. God is declaring that His power today is not demonstrated in man's wisdom, or even in signs and miracles. It is rooted in the changed lives of those who hear the message of the cross, bow down before the Savior, and receive Him. That can produce a test-tube miracle of change that even the most skeptically blind cannot fail to recognize.

Most Christians wish that God would somehow demonstrate His power so effectively that any doubter would be forced to admit His presence in our universe. But at this point in time, that does not seem to be God's plan. As Luke 16:29 says, "They have Moses and the prophets [the Bible]; let them hear them." God continues to perform miracles today, but they are not what I call "test-tube miracles"—that is, those so astounding that even an atheist would have to acknowledge God's powerful hand at work. Instead, He has chosen to provide a pair of tools for impelling people to believe in Him: the Word of God and the power of the cross, which demonstrates itself in the changed lives of new believers.

When a prostitute, drug addict, homosexual, nymphomaniac, or hardened criminal receives Christ and begins to live a changed life, that is the power of the cross demonstrated in human shoe leather. Many people have been converted by witnessing such transformations, for no other power on earth could have changed that person. This complete transformation should not surprise us, for on the basis of 2 Corinthians 5:17 we should expect it.

> If anyone is in Christ, he is a new creation; old things have passed away; behold, all things have become new.

## Illustration of the Power of the Cross

Charles Colson, formerly of Watergate fame, is now even better known by his shift in life and ministry to hardened criminals in prisons throughout the country. He was formerly Special Assistant to the President of the United States, with an office in the White House, but since his conversion, the power of the cross has elevated him to a more exalted position. I remember telling an attorney friend who was close to the Nixon administration about Colson's conversion shortly after it was reported. He sat straight up and exclaimed, "Impossible!" Then he made a derogatory statement about Colson's life and character. We agreed to wait and see. Time has proved my friend wrong. The Scripture that declares "Nothing is impossible with God" has again been validated.

But that illustration can be taken one step further. Prison Fellowship, the ministry that Chuck Colson founded, along with Bill Glass' prison ministry in Texas and other similar ministries to prisoners, displays the same phenomenon. Of those criminals who have a genuine conversion experience and are discipled in the Word of God, more than 85 percent never return to prison. If you know anything about the discouraging recidivism record (the return of hardened criminals after their release for committing additional crimes), you are aware that 85 percent *do* return to prison. What makes the difference? The power of the cross!

The addiction to hard drugs can be subjected to the same test. A friend of mine has a ministry to teenage drug users. He tells me that the best government programs, even those awash in money, achieve only a 15 percent success rate of young people staying off drugs after release. But in his program that takes the kids to camp, introduces them to a conversion experience with Jesus Christ, helps them medically kick the drug habit, and disciples them in the Word of God, only 15 percent return to the use of drugs.

Even more graphic results become visible when the power of the cross transforms homosexuals. The only agency in the country which effectively induces homosexuals to change their lifestyle is the church of Jesus Christ. That change starts with the gospel offer of a conversion experience.

Homosexuality is probably the most binding vice that can grip any human being. It is so binding that most secular counselors are powerless to help even those who want to become heterosexual. Several years ago I was interviewed with a Los Angeles psychiatrist on an open-mike radio talk show about homosexuality. He evidently became threatened when I maintained that I had seen 30 homosexuals who had rejected that lifestyle after accepting Christ as their Savior. First he accused me of lying. Then he confessed the impotence of his profession. "I have been a practicing psychiatrist for 33 years, and I have never seen a homosexual change; furthermore, I don't know any other counselor in the Los Angeles basin that has either."

That is a tragic confession, particularly in a day when over 70 percent of those who contract AIDS are homosexuals. One would judge that the threat of an early, painful death would cause any person to give up an unhealthy lifestyle, but the great influence exercised by homosexuality over the individual seems unbreakable. Yet many have come out of that lifestyle after accepting Christ.

When I told that story on another open-mike show in San Francisco, I was of course challenged by the homosexuals who called in. (Many were less than polite.) That night, after I had preached in a large church in the area, a couple waited after my message to share with me their family secret. As I was shaking hands with the husband, the wife blurted, "Pastor LaHaye, you are now looking at number 31 who has come out of that lifestyle." There they stood, he holding a four-month-old baby as she grasped the hand of their two-year-old. He had come to Christ in that church over four years before. Then they had met, fallen in love, and married. I have told that story several times and at last count shook hands with self-acknowledged "number 48." The power of the cross is undeniable.

During a recent election in Vermont as I campaigned for a Christian candidate, a handsome young father with an absolutely beautiful wife asked if he could hug me. Then he recounted that reading my book *THE UNHAPPY GAYS: What Everyone Should Know About Homosexuality* was used of God to lead him to Christ ten years before. "Now I am an evangelist, and part of my ministry is to homosexuals." And he is not alone. Over 50 ministries, including Exodus International, some with chapters in every state of the union, specialize in leading homosexuals out of that lifestyle. Each has its own counseling technique, but all have the same source of power—the cross of Christ.

## It Was the Same in the First Century

This should come as no surprise to the Christian who knows his Bible. Note carefully the following Scripture:

> Do you not know that the unrighteous will not inherit the kingdom of God? Do not be deceived. Neither fornicators, nor idolaters, nor adulterers, nor homosexuals, nor sodomites, nor thieves, nor covetous, nor drunkards, nor revilers, nor extortioners will inherit the kingdom of God. And such were some of you. But you were washed, but you were sanctified, but you were justified in the name of the Lord Jesus and by the Spirit of our God (1 Corinthians 6:9-11).

Paul records an astonishing list of sins which had enslaved these Corinthians before they experienced the power of the cross. They had been fornicators, idolaters, adulterers, homosexuals, revilers, drunkards, extortionists—and the list goes on. The New Testament converts were not goody-goodies just waiting for Paul and the apostles to approach them with the gospel. Admittedly, a few were like the centurion in Acts 10 and the Ethiopian eunuch, but most of the early church Christians can best be described as degenerates before they were loosed from the power of darkness and introduced to the power of the cross.

Consider carefully the names of the churches to which Paul wrote: Colossians, Galatians, Ephesians, Corinthians. Each city was a citadel of moral depravity. Because of their pagan religions, these people in their unsaved days had been introduced into sexual vices that usually maintain a lifetime grip on individuals, shortening their lives. Paul said, "Such *were* some of you." But now that they had come to the cross, they were changed—"washed . . . sanctified . . . justified in the name of the Lord Jesus and by the Spirit of our God."

In his letter to the Colossians, Paul challenged the believers to "put to death . . . fornication, uncleanness, passion, evil desire, and covetousness"—some of the most gripping habits to which a person can fall prey on this earth. Where did he expect them to get the power for such a change of lifestyle? From the same place God expects us to receive it—the power of the cross, the indwelling Holy Spirit, and the Word of God.

## Summary

If you are a Christian, you have within yourself the capacity for change. No matter what your temperament combination, family background, or experiences, you have the power to modify your life. You may be selfish, short-tempered, inconsiderate, unloving, critical, demanding, fearful, or sexually misdirected, but as a Christian you now have at your disposal the divine power of a life-renovating God.

If you are not a Christian, you lack that power. As much as you may wish to overcome your weaknesses, you cannot begin to march down the road of renewal without His power. Take the first step by praying the sinner's prayer, "Lord, be merciful to me a sinner," and personally invite Jesus Christ to come into your heart as your Lord and Savior. Formally, in an act of prayer, give your life to Him, and then let Him take control of your life. Once you have uttered that prayer by faith, you are ready to demonstrate that you are "a new creature" for whom "old things are passed away and all things are become new" (including temperament weaknesses). As we shall see in Section Two of this book, the process is neither automatic nor easy. But since you are now attached to the divine source of power, all things are possible. According to Dr. Henry Brandt, "You can use your background (including your temperament) as an excuse for present behavior only until you become a Christian. After that it is no longer a valid excuse."

# *Other Differences*

During the past few years the feminist movement has intimidated many people from admitting the obvious: Men and women are different. We saw this on the evening news almost every night during the Persian Gulf conflict. Some women soldiers were filmed as mechanics working on air-planes and trucks in the Saudi Desert; others (such as heli-copter pilots) were about as close to combat situations as women could get. In fact, two female pilots were shot down. Liberals in Congress (particularly some Congresswomen) will not be satisfied until women come home in body bags just like the men. They refuse to face the fact that men and women are profoundly different.

We are not suggesting that women are inferior to men—just different. In fact, in some areas women are supe-rior. In his book *Straight Talk to Men and Their Wives,* Dr. James Dobson offers these insights:

> Males and females differ anatomically, sexually, emo-tionally, psychologically, and biochemically. We differ in literally every cell of our bodies, for each sex carries a unique chromosomal pattern. Much is written today about so-called sex-change operations, whereby males

are transformed into females or vice versa. Admittedly, it is possible to alter the external genitalia by surgery, and silicone can be used to pad the breasts or round out a bony frame. Hormones can then be injected to feminize or masculinize the convert. But nothing can be done to change the assignment of sex made by God at the instant of conception. That determination is carried in each cell, and it will read "male" or "female" from the earliest moment of life to the point of death. The Bible says emphatically, "Male *and* female created he them" (Genesis 1:27 KJV, emphasis added). Not one sex, but *two!*

Furthermore, it is my deep conviction that each sex displays unique emotional characteristics that are genetically endowed. Cultural influences cannot account for these novelties. Few psychologists have had the courage to express this view in recent years, because the women's movement has perceived it as insulting. But to be *different* from men does not make women *inferior* to men. Males and females are original creations of God, each bearing strengths and weaknesses that counterbalance and interface with one another. It is a beautiful design that must not be disassembled.[1]

Dr. Dobson then draws attention to the most significant physical difference between men and women—the menstrual cycle. This difference is not just physical, for it involves the total woman and, through her, influences the husband. During that time she goes through an emotional and psychological as well as a physical change. Some women even experience spiritual crisis. That is, they can be secure in the knowledge of God and His salvation until their periods come, and then the insecurity of the believer takes over, mainly because they are uncertain at that time about many things. Dr. Dobson beautifully compares a woman's monthly cycle to the seasons of the year.

It has been said, quite accurately, that the four weeks of the menstrual cycle are characteristic of the four seasons of the year. The first week after a period can be termed the springtime of the physiological calendar. New estrogens (female hormones) are released each day and a woman's body begins to rebound from the recent winter.

The second week represents the summertime of the cycle, when the living is easy. A woman during this phase has more self-confidence than during any other phase of the month. It is a time of maximum energy, enthusiasm, amiability, and self-esteem. Estrogen levels account for much of this optimism, reaching a peak during mid-cycle, when ovulation occurs. The relationship between husband and wife is typically at its best during these days of summer, when sexual desire (and the potential for pregnancy) are paramount.

But alas, the fall must surely follow summer. Estrogen levels steadily dwindle as the woman's body prepares itself for another period of menstruation. A second hormone, called progesterone, is released, which reduces the effect of estrogen and initiates the symptoms of premenstrual tension. It is a bleak phase of the month. Self-esteem deteriorates day by day, bringing depression and pessimism with it. A bloated and sluggish feeling often produces not only discomfort but also the belief that "I am ugly." Irritability and aggression become increasingly evident as the week progresses, reaching a climax immediately prior to menstruation.

Then comes the winter and the period of the menstrual flow. Women differ remarkably in intensity of these symptoms, but most experience some discomfort. Those most vulnerable even find it necessary to spend a day or two in bed during the winter season, suffering from cramping and generalized misery. Gradually, the siege passes and the refreshing newness of springtime returns.[2]

This unique difference is selected to emphasize that men and women function in dissimilar ways; they feel and think differently for a very good reason: They *are* different! The degree or expression of that difference will vary depending on the woman's temperament. But if the contrast between the sexes is not taken into account, it will complicate the adjustment process. It is best to accept it. After all, we are attracted to the opposite sex because of differences.

## Even Our Brains Are Different

Modern research has uncovered the fact that the brains of men and women are not fully comparable. "The new research is producing a complex picture of the brain in which differences in anatomical structure seem to lead to advantages in performance on certain mental tasks."[3] It is suggested that these physical differences in the brain could very well account for variations that show up each year on SAT scores.

While these differences are still the subject of intense controversy, most researchers agree that women generally show advantages over men in certain verbal abilities. For instance, on average, girls begin to speak earlier than boys and women are more fluent with words than men, and make fewer mistakes in grammar and pronunciation.

On the other hand, men on average tend to be better than women on certain spatial tasks, such as drawing maps of places they have been and rotating imagined geometric images in their mind's eye—a skill useful in mathematics, engineering, and architecture.

Of course, the advantages for each sex are only on average. There are individual men who do as well as the best women on verbal tests, and women who do as well as the best men on spatial tasks.[4]

In short, we now recognize two major differences between men and women—one their sexuality, the other the size and function of their brain. Further research may uncover other significant variants, but these two, which influence almost every other organ in our bodies, could well account for the many differences between men and women which in marriage often cause great dissension.

## Major Sources of Conflict Between the Sexes

A recent study on the conflicts between men and women was done by Dr. David M. Buss at the University of Michigan. Considered "the most sophisticated study yet conducted," it encompassed 600 men and women. Dr. Buss identified 147 distinct sources of conflict between men and women. While both men and women generally shared their dislike for infidelity, they differed in priority on most other subjects. The following provides an abbreviated list of their objections.

## What Bothers a Woman About a Man

*Infidelity:* Most women (before it occurs) insist that they cannot forgive it.

*Sexual Demands:* Making her feel sexually used; trying to force sex or demanding it.

*Condescension:* Ignoring her opinions because she is a woman; treating her as inferior or stupid; making her feel inadequate.

*Emotional Constriction and Excess:* Hiding his emotions to act tough; drinking or smoking too much.

*Neglect:* Unreliability; not spending enough time with her or calling when promised; ignoring her feelings or failing to say he loves her.

*Thoughtlessness:* Being unmannerly—belching, for instance, or leaving the toilet seat up; not helping to clean up the home; teasing her about how long it takes to get dressed.

## What Bothers a Man About a Woman

*Sexual Rejection:* Refusing to have sex; being unresponsive to sexual advances; being a sexual tease.

*Moodiness:* Acting "bitchy" or otherwise being out of sorts.

*Self-Absorption:* Fussing over her appearance, worrying about her face and hair; spending too much on clothes.[5]

## My Own Observations

The findings of Dr. Buss and his associates mirror my own observations as I work with thousands of couples each year who attend my two-day Family Seminars. During the question-and-answer session, the audience is invited to submit written questions, to which I verbally respond. The following list reflects the sources of conflict or disillusionment among the largely Christian couples with whom I work.

## What Wives Object to Most About Husbands

*1. He is too aggressive sexually.*

The sexual needs of men and women usually show up near the end of the first year of marriage or after the first child. The initial year becomes so exciting that most wives can keep up with their young husband's sexual desires. (Yet a bride of three months asked me recently, "How long should I expect him to want sex every day?" Another inquired, "Is four times in one day abnormal?")

Usually, after the first year most couples come together in the physical expression of their love about three times a week, depending largely on the wife's monthly cycle. The difference is not so much frequency as timing and emotional expression. A woman likes romance. She prefers multiple expressions of tenderness and love, even kisses and touching over the course of the evening. Then she delights in climaxing a romantic evening with lovemaking.

A loving husband may want to accommodate her, but his emotional motor can zoom from zero to 60 miles per hour in less than five seconds. So unless he is willing to practice self-control, she feels that she is fighting him off all evening. That difference must be dealt with unselfishly. Sometimes the wife should submit to his instant flash desire, but most of the time he should cool his jets and learn to be a romancer. The wife should certainly beware of putting him off all evening and then using "tiredness" as an excuse to send him to sleep unfulfilled. She could possibly catch a nap during the late afternoon/evening or make love earlier in the evening.

Metabolism is a culprit here. That is, early-bird "wrens" often marry late-night "owls." A person's sexual interest naturally follows his metabolism. Early birds are more interested in love during the morning hours, whereas owls are more excitable at night.

Dr. Buss' scientific study and my observations through the years agree that sexual expression is enormously significant. Historically it has been the purpose of marriage. But couples must learn to accommodate each other's needs and interests. The key to sexual satisfaction, which is not very complex, can be achieved in three simple steps.

1) Study the subject by reading at least two books: *The Act of Marriage* by this author and *Intended for Pleasure* by Dr. Ed Wheat, a medical doctor. All couples need to know about their own sexuality and certainly that of their partner.

2) Communicate honestly and frequently with your partner about your sexual needs and feelings. Major warning: The most difficult subject in the world for most couples to discuss is sex, particularly if they lack a vibrant sex life. In fact, in order to determine whether a couple has a dynamic love life, one need only determine whether it is easy for him or her to discuss the subject. One woman confessed that she and her husband "had not discussed their sex life in 25 years." It should not be surprising that intimacy was not fulfilling to either of them. When you are not in the mood, say so up-front and honestly rather than lead your partner on. Good communication is essential.

3) Out of unselfish love, try to accommodate your partner's needs. Your most important sex organ is your brain. If in the spirit of love you tell yourself "I can," then you can. But if you declare "I can't," your brain will turn off your glands and you can't. Selfishness not only destroys love but kills its expression—for both of you.

## 2. He won't help around the house.

We have already noted the result of the *USA TODAY* survey that 82 percent of the women whose husbands helped around the house "would marry the same man all over again"—which is 33 percent above the national average of women who would select the same spouse. That is awesome evidence that such a gesture has a profound effect on a woman. Most of all, it demonstrates that her work is important and that her husband cares about her. The wife can make this point clear to her husband, but he is the one who needs to act thoughtfully in this regard.

## 3. He is not the spiritual leader of the home.

Women tend to be idealists more than men, and a Christian woman usually dreams that her husband will serve in the role prescribed by Scripture—priest of the home. Few wives object when their husband leads in family devotions, church attendance as a family, or prayer together as a couple. Many are disillusioned when he does not.

*4. He doesn't show respect for me or my views.*

Buss called it "condescending," and he is right on target. Women are more emotional and intuitive, whereas men tend to be logical thinkers whose emotions (except for marriage and buying a car) do not dominate when decisions are made (within the limits of their temperament, of course). That does not make a man's decisions better than a woman's. He may take the wrong path via "logic," and she may make the right decision via "feelings." They often clash, however, because of the means by which they arrive at their decisions.

For example, when a husband asks, "Why did you buy that dress?" it is suicide for a woman to reply, "I was depressed as I walked through the mall, but when I saw this dress and bought it, I felt much better." He can't understand that! He doesn't recognize that she was responding to feeling and intuition. It would be better for her to say, "I haven't had a new dress for six months and needed one for the party next Friday night. I spotted this one on sale for 30 percent off and bought it." Seldom will he argue about that—not because the reasoning is persuasive, but because she could offer a rational "method for her madness," which is logical.

A wife cannot stand ridicule, particularly by her husband! Disagreement or debate, yes, but ridicule becomes a cruel whip to a wife. It belligerently asserts, "You are a stupid woman!" Such thoughts should never be transmitted verbally. A wise man finds areas in which he can brag about his wife's intelligence and abilities. As he does so, he will enhance her confidence and, as a result, will uncover even more positive qualities. Because a woman gains her self-acceptance from her husband, he should make it a point to build her up, not tear her down, particularly in front of the children or friends.

### 5. *He doesn't discipline the children properly.*

Some husbands leave all the effort of child correction to the wife, but the objection may apply to the angry father who disciplines his children in wrath. Almost all discipline done in anger is dangerous—too much, too hard, begotten of a malicious spirit. Because correction should instruct rather than antagonize, it should never be driven by negative emotions. Anything less than loving reproof is mere punishment.

In addition, discipline should be a joint venture. That is, partners must agree on the rules and their enforcement. And if the parent who witnesses "the crime" inflicts the punishment, the father does not have to become the giant monster who punishes as soon as he walks in the door. Mother should be up-to-date on her discipline when he comes home, allowing Dad to take over at that point. Above all, the father should teach, lead, and (if necessary) demand respect for Mother from the children.

The man who works out his frustrations toward his wife by indulging his children when they need discipline is not only destroying his marital relationship but subverting his offspring. While it is true that the Bible specifically instructs the wife to respect her husband (Ephesians 5:33), it is difficult to believe that a man can love his wife (same verse) without consistently demonstrating respect.

### 6. *All my husband ever thinks about is his job and sports.*

It is an acknowledged fact that men, particularly as they get older, are often preoccupied with vocational thoughts. Part of that is intuitive. Since God has made him the provider for the family, he will naturally think long and often about his work, career, future, and family security. We would label him irresponsible if he didn't. By contrast, the wife tends to be a "nester," the natural result of her maternal nurturing intuition. For that reason, a woman may exercise more interest in the color of the kitchen, the style of the drapes, or the quality of the carpet. Husbands need to enter into these discussions by letting the wife make the final decisions about the home. After all, she spends more time there, and besides, the home is more a reflection of her than of her mate.

In love, they need to learn to share their honest thoughts and feelings about both home and vocation. That is, just as a husband should force himself to become more concerned with household matters, a wife should compel herself to show greater interest in and knowledge of her husband's profession, whether or not she has a vocation of her own outside the home. The more areas of commonality a couple can create between them, the more time they can spend talking and sharing. That is called bonding. Couples who are well-bonded can talk about everything.

Yes, most men are sports freaks, but I urge wives to join them. Learn the basic rules of the game, ask leading questions, and enter into your husband's center of attraction. Don't say, "I don't like football." Instead, ask yourself, "Do I understand the game?" Remember, what we *like* least in life is what we *know* the least about. My wife hated football until she learned to understand the crucial third-down play. Now we have football parties whenever possible, and she will complain, "You'll have to help me get ready (the refreshments) so I can watch the game too." And yes, I helped "get ready" for Super Bowl, even though driving to the supermarket and cutting vegetable strips are not my favorite pastimes. But very honestly, I want to keep her a fan of the game. Besides, I love her! Here is our motto for partner sports preference: "If you can't cure 'em, then join 'em."

## What Husbands Object to Most About Wives

Wives are not alone in voicing complaints about their husbands; men register their discontent equally. Here is my prioritized list of basic objections.

### 1. My wife is undersexed.

The usual complaint is based on frequency difference. In most marriages, the husband expects lovemaking more often than the wife. Instead of asking married couples how often they would *like* to make love, my survey asked, "How often *do* you make love?" Since I had the couples separated by age groups in decade intervals, I was intrigued to find that wives almost invariably indicated that they made love more frequently than did their husbands. Why? Husbands spend more time thinking about it and craving it than their wives. Because the sex drive is generally stronger in men than in women, it is more important to them. My unscientific impression from analyzing the results of my survey suggests that, depending on her age, the average Christian wife would score her sex life very satisfactory if she made love one to four times a month. Most men would prefer one to four times a week (depending, of course, on their age).

In fairness, this difference is not always due to the sex drive. It may reflect the serious differences mentioned above. Lovemaking to a man is an intensely physical occasion. To a woman it is primarily an emotional experience. True, her orgasm is just as physically satisfying (and necessary) as a man's, but to achieve it, she must dedicate a longer period of time to warming up and cooling down. A woman does not like to be "used physically" to satisfy a husband's lust. Sex should never be something a man "does" to his wife but an experience they share together, providing them the greatest single pleasure that they can enjoy throughout their entire lifetime. It is a gift of God, meant for our good. But to be all that it should be, we must enter into it unselfishly, seeking our partner's satisfaction more than our own. Show me two lovers who are primarily interested in providing fulfillment and pleasure to each other, and I will show you two people who enjoy an extremely satisfying sex life. And whatever the frequency, it will create mutual bliss.

A NOTE TO MEN: If I had my book *The Act of Marriage* to write over again, I would add that husbands should spend anywhere from five to ten or more minutes longer in foreplay building up to the ACT, and 15 minutes to an hour in "afterglow" whenever possible. A man usually has to learn the art of cooling down, because after ejaculation his emotions drop instantly to 44 degrees below zero. His wife's, however, do not. She still enjoys the tenderness and touching of afterglow. To her that is almost as satisfying as the orgasmic explosion. Adapting to her emotional mood will help the husband convey that he loves *her*—not just her body. To a woman that is extremely important.

*2. My wife is too critical.*

Frequently men add, "My wife nitpicks me to death." As we have seen, Melancholies are more analytical than others, and women are more critical than men, generally speaking. It may be related to their maternal instinct as the nurturer of the young, but it is maddening to a husband.

Wifely criticism stifles conversation! Wives commonly complain in the counseling room, "My husband never talks to me about his work, his friends, his life—nothing." But they forget to add that the husband usually responds, "Why should I share with you? You criticize everything I say." And reduced to its simplest terms, that is why two lovers quit talking. Before marriage, young lovers can chatter endlessly about everything—or nothing. But after marriage, women tend to level criticism at the way the husband drives, eats, cuts the lawn, tends his closet, cleans his desk, and takes care of the garage. Frankly, none of us likes criticism, and we like it even less from the person we love. If criticism turns to harping, or if it shakes his self-confidence, he will soon refuse to hold a conversation.

It is a wise partner who never criticizes in a demeaning manner. Suggestions can be given tactfully. Men usually like to talk out their ideas—not for advice or criticism but for clarification. Helpful suggestions are beneficial, but criticism is resented. When a man trots out his goals and plans, he does not want them nailed like a target to the wall. If his partner starts shooting darts into them, he soon moves the target. I have regularly noticed that the woman who steals another's husband never engages in dissecting his dreams and goals; she is a listener.

### 3. My wife spends too much money.

You have no doubt heard the old expression, "My wife and I are having a lifetime contest to see if I can make money faster than she can spend it. So far she's winning." Many couples fight over money and spending habits. The best remedy is to establish a budget and follow it. While deficit spending may temporarily help the economy, it places an unnecessary burden on the family. If spending is a problem, sit down and discuss it frankly. In the budget, if at all possible, something should be entered for both husband and wife to spend as they see fit—something they do not have to account for. Otherwise both should stay within the budget. When a crisis arises, they should talk it through prayerfully and come to a joint understanding.

The credit card is a very dangerous incentive to overspending. If you cannot control it, destroy it. What determines whether you are in control? Quite simply, if you have to pay interest on the use of the card, you need to exercise "scissors management." Most credit card companies offer free use of the card for the first 30 days, and earn their money from a small percentage charged to the merchant. The retailer is willing to pay it because it provides him instant income, and he knows that more people will buy if credit is available. But after 30 days, trouble begins to arise in River City. An exorbitant interest rate that should be deemed illegal is added to the statement, and many people begin to fall hopelessly behind. Don't let that happen to you. Financial pressures put needless burdens on a marriage, inhibiting adjustment and creating unnecessary conflict.

*4. My wife is too moody and emotional.*

Measured by maleness, the husband may be right—but women are not men. They are special creatures of God who, generally speaking, are more emotional than their counterparts. That does not make them inferior—just different. It is a happy woman who marries a mature, sensitive man who realizes that every 28 days, through no fault of her own (and so they can share the making of children someday), she will experience an enormous mood swing. Her mood may last two days or as long as ten. While bearing children may lessen the physical pain, it does not always curtail the severity or length of the moods. A man should learn to live with such emotional alterations—first by noting them on his calendar in order to anticipate them, and then by being as loving and understanding as possible, ready to share her pain seasons as well as her spring and summer seasons.

Evidence that women are more emotional than men (if you need such evidence) appears in a three-year study released in December 1990 by the American Psychological Association.

> ... Women are twice as likely as men to suffer from major depression ... which afflicts about 7 million American women, leads to 30,000 suicides annually and costs society an estimated $16 billion a year, the researchers said. The illness has been known for some time to strike women disproportionately ...

evidence gathered by the researchers suggested that the sexual differences in the incidence of depression were real and that the particular problems facing women have been unappreciated by the medical profession. . . .

The task force's principal finding is that no single factor is responsible for the dramatically higher rates of major depression among women. Nor, the report said, is the difference due entirely to simple biological differences between men and women. In fact, menstruation, pregnancy, abortion, and menopause were found to be only modestly associated with severe emotional distress.

Infertility, however, was a major risk factor, with 40 percent of women in one study reporting that their inability to conceive was "the most upsetting experience of their lives."

Other key risk factors for women identified by the report were:

*Cognitive and personality styles.* Women are more prone to avoidant, passive, dependent behavior patterns and pessimistic, negative thought processes and are more likely than men to focus on depressed feelings rather than developing "action and mastery strategies."

*Marriage and children.* Married women are three times more likely than either married men or single women to be depressed in an unhappy marriage, with vulnerability to depression increasing as the number of children increases and the age of the children decreases. Women with more and younger children are more depressed than those with fewer and older children.

*Sexual and physical abuse.* New evidence suggests that victimization of women may be more prevalent than previously thought, and, as a result, may play an underappreciated role in promoting depression.[6]

The above passage suggests that monthly mood swings do not make women more emotionally gifted than men, but most women—particularly Melancholies, Sanguines, and Phlegmatics—are more emotionally expressive than men. It is a sign of emotional depth. It certainly is appropriate to "weep with those that weep," and even Jesus wept. So a wife should never be faulted for showing her emotions—or for that matter teased unduly if she feels self-conscious. A woman at times enters adulthood with false feelings of inferiority because she was taunted unmercifully by brothers or possibly a father who was ignorant of her needs. Just because events that cause a man to fight will make a girl or woman cry does not mean that her emotional state is unstable! It simply indicates that she is a normal female—and should be treated so.

Personally, I am not a weeper, though many times I have wished I were. My tear ducts seemed to dry up when I was 12, shortly after my father died, and I have never wept since. But I admire those who can show their true feelings of compassion for others. We emotional spastics just break out in hives, or else turn our cowardly hearts away from emotionally hurting people. Sometimes the only demonstration of support that adequately ministers to people is emotional expression.

One final word of advice to a man whose wife is emotionally demonstrative: Thank God, protect her when she is emotionally vulnerable, try not to be the cause of her emotional pain, and never make fun of her tears. The woman who can freely shed tears is usually free to express all kinds of emotions—some that you can't live without.

## Other Areas of Difference

What man has not exclaimed, "I will never understand women!" That is because he thinks vocationally as a God-assigned provider, whereas she responds as a "nester" or homemaker, for God has assigned her the job of mothering. Consequently she possesses the intuition and instincts necessary to perform her tasks well. And the list goes on.

If we add differences in temperament, plus the traditions and training they both received (good or bad) as they were growing up, plus the parental love (or lack of it) showered upon them, plus their life experiences, and most of all their spiritual motivations and genuine commitment to God's will, the total sum will explain why two people can love each other dearly yet be so different.

Married partners, then, must admit to the following: 1) Being different is normal; 2) living in a world of contrasts isn't all bad, for it insures variety; 3) admittedly, differences produce conflict; 4) they need not be fatal to any marriage, no matter how serious; 5) with God's help, two people who are different but complementary can learn to live happily ever after—if they want to.

# PART TWO

# How to Adjust to Your Opposite Partner

# The Art of Adjustment

Now that we know that opposites are attracted to each other because of the good impression made by their different strengths, it is time to examine why these same opposites are often repelled by each other after marriage, and what they can do about the problem.

By this time you must realize that no one possesses 100 percent strengths. That would reflect the perfect man or woman, and the Bible clearly states, "There is none righteous, no, not one." It also says, "All have sinned and come short of the glory of God." By nature we are all a combination of both strengths and weaknesses, and, as we have seen, it is our weaknesses that get us into trouble. A couple's opposite weaknesses may even cause them to fall out of love.

There are two reasons for that: 1) Opposing weaknesses create clashes, from personality collisions to conflicts of will, ambition, desire, and drive; 2) it is difficult to accept another person's weakness when it falls into your area of strength. If both partners exhibit weaknesses in the same areas, they usually find it easy to be accepting and understanding of these weaknesses. But when one is weak where the other is strong, the "tower of strength" may look down on "the wimp of weakness" and even become contemptuous because the partner indulges such weaknesses.

True love, as we shall see, is not conditional. That is, it does not promise, "As long as you are perfect, I will love you." Instead, true love is not affected by a partner's behavior; it endures regardless of positive or negative treatment.

Even so, adjustment to an opposite partner is not automatic; it is an art. The following chapters are dedicated to helping you develop that art.

# Giant Step One
# in Marital Adjustment

At the close of a lively Phil Donahue show on the breakdown of marriage, he received the signal that only 30 seconds of the program remained. Turning to me, he asked, "Dr. LaHaye, can you in one word sum up the major cause of divorce today?" "Yes," I said, "the big word SELFISHNESS!" Readily agreeing, Phil then inquired, "But isn't everyone selfish to some extent?"

I considered that one of Donahue's more perceptive observations, for all people *are* selfish to some extent, depending on their temperament and childhood training. And the degree to which one overcomes that problem determines the success and happiness of his marriage. Some people select a marriage partner for all the wrong reasons and introduce their selfish agenda into the new union, destroying interpersonal skills and soon erasing all feelings of love.

It is almost humanly impossible to love a compulsively selfish person. I have noticed in my associations with three- and four-time divorcees that they are very selfish people; one disastrous experience is followed by another, and all are blamed on the other party. They seem incapable of recognizing the selfish culprit.

## Everyone Is Somewhat Selfish

To one degree or another, Donahue was right: Almost everyone prefers himself before others. Egotism is induced by our temperament, then either increased or decreased depending on childhood training, love (or lack of it), youthful experiences, education, and other factors. Each temperament has its own way of expressing it, but all have the problem to some extent. We often consider a person raised as an only child as being more selfish and a greater marriage risk than others because he has not learned to share with other children during his maturing years. That may explain why children from large families often experience a lower divorce rate than mates who were only children.

Nothing is more destructive to a marriage than selfishness. "I insist on having my own way!" "I want the last word!" "I can spend our money as I please!" "But I wanted to vacation in the mountains this summer!" "I" problems create a myopic marriage partner. Selfish people are rigid and intolerant of other people's desires, insensitive to other's needs or feelings.

The diagram on the next page shows the varying degrees of selfishness, noted by the increasing size of the "S" seated on the throne of the will.

According to this diagram, some people are more egocentric than others. For that reason a few non-Christians are able to effect a happy marriage without God's help. They seem to get lucky in the selection process, gaining a partner who is only normally selfish; consequently the two may adjust properly to each other. But the compulsively selfish person, for whatever reason, is always a matrimonial risk. Frankly, I know of no power on earth that can turn a selfish person into a loving, compassionate, "others-conscious" individual except a genuine conversion experience, and even then one

Normally
selfish

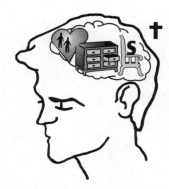

Self-
absorbed

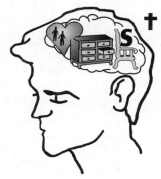

Compulsively
selfish

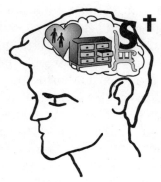

# Varying Degrees of Selfishness
# (Non-Christians)

Diagram 2: Degrees of Selfishness

must cooperate with the Spirit of God to receive and develop the spirit of unselfishness that God alone can provide.

## What Is Selfishness?

A selfish person thinks first, last, and always of himself. Such an attitude appears most clearly in his conversation and conduct, particularly in his home, the central arena of life. It may likewise reveal itself in one's work and recreational life, marring all interpersonal relationships. In short, selfishness is the opposite of love.

Babies are the epitome of selfishness. When they come home from the hospital, they never consider making an appointment with Mother for their first night's feeding. Instead, they wait until she is in a deep sleep, still exhausted from giving birth, then pierce the night silence with a shriek for food—not ten minutes from now, but right this second!

We understand and accept that—in babies. But when the same child is 21 years old and still demands that his needs and wants be met immediately, we label him selfish. Such individuals are always a marital risk. Anyone considering marriage should carefully examine his prospective partner's treatment of others, especially family members, for consideration of other people becomes a significant indicator of future marital harmony.

I am often asked, "How old do you have to be to get married?" The answer has nothing to do with age. An 18- or 20-year-old may be mature enough for marriage, and I have met people in their eighties who were too immature (or selfish) to marry. One is not old enough for matrimony until he is unselfish enough to think more of someone else's needs and desires than his own. Such individuals rarely divorce and usually enjoy a happy marriage, regardless of contrasting temperaments or other differences that may exist between them. Conflicts in taste or attitude do not destroy marital harmony. By contrast, expressions of self-ishness are lethal.

## What Causes Selfishness?

The first contributing cause of selfishness emanates from the gene pool of our parents in the form of tempera-ment—an inevitable part of the Adamic nature resulting from the fall. How our parents loved and disciplined us (or failed to do so) in youth will have a profound effect on the degree of selfishness that temperament engenders. Thus two people of identical temperament may reflect varying degrees of selfishness when they grow up. Behavior, we must remember, depends on many things, including tem-perament, childhood training and love, life experience, and spiritual maturity.

Sanguines are natural-born egotists. The thought that everyone doesn't love them never occurs to them. They like to be the center of attraction, captivating other people with their endless conversation. But if you listen to their talk long enough, you will discover that they are their own favorite person. Most of what they say revolves around their interests and desires. They are driven by a need to gain the approval of others. Even when they break their wedding vows, self-indulgence never impels them to consider the trauma experienced by their partner until it is too late. Unselfish Sanguines are rare. Only the Spirit-filled life can modify this temperament.

Cholerics are subject to compulsive selfishness. They know they are right (even when they are wrong) and never hesitate to impose their will on others. Having little need for the approval of others, they really don't care how demanding and unsympathetic they are. Insensitive to friends and associates, they will seldom try to hide their self-ishness. One reason they have so few lasting friends is that they are so self-centered and unreasonably demanding of all their acquaintances.

Frequently absorbed with themselves, Melancholies often marry to allow someone else to fulfill their needs (real or imagined); no one can do that, we must admit, and consequently they become unhappy soon after the wedding. Of course, they weren't really happy *before* the wedding. Any doctor will tell you that more of his active patients are Melancholy than any other temperament. The moment they feel a pain, all thoughts are turned inward. The world must stop until the discomfort is alleviated, but they usually encounter other distresses en route to solving the first.

In extreme cases they have been known to assume the fetal position, reflecting their desire to return to the one time in life when they felt safe and every need was met by another person. Such people, unless they learn to be "others-conscious," are difficult to live with. They read into everything you say and assume you are attacking or criticizing them, when in reality you may not even be thinking of them. But don't admit that; it would be considered an insult. They are almost impossible to please. Fortunately, the Spirit of God can help to overcome the selfishness of a Melancholy!

Phlegmatics are usually pleasant marriage partners because they are so nice, gentle, and diplomatic; they don't tend to express their selfish impulses freely. Introverts by nature, they are afraid of the consequences if they were to voice or act out selfish desires. Their selfishness is easiest to perceive in their handling of finances and in their extensive self-protective devices. Sheltering themselves at all costs, they seldom expose fears and hesitations. For that reason they rarely accept opportunities to perform in public. They would rather sit on their talent than risk ridicule or embarrassment, and they often limit their family and partner from getting involved in worthwhile activities or businesses due to their obsession with self-protection. A gentle disposition makes a Phlegmatic easier to live with than other types, but he and his partner would be much happier if they would let the Spirit of God overcome self-ishness.

Christian psychologist David Field in his book *Marriage Personalities* introduces two principal causes of selfishness: 1) egotism and 2) low self-esteem. He claims that both are "a serious problem in many marriages."

Egotistical people, he explains, are narcissistic, seeking to draw excessive amounts of attention to themselves. Often they put others down in an attempt to promote themselves. "They insist that their viewpoint is always right."[7]

> Egotists have a tough time in marriage. Their inter-ests tend to be in outside activities, such as job and hobbies, rather than in the home. This doesn't mean that they don't care about the marriage, but rather that they derive more fulfillment from their accomplishments than from their relationships.
>
> The most obvious example of egotism is Mr. Macho in the Macho marriage. Most Active-Resistant mar-riages also have an egotistic partner in the resistant role. I have occasionally told egocentric partners that they are a lot like a rock in a blender. To them, anyone who does not fit in with their plans is a source of irritation.
>
> The egotist has several fears which influence his lack of trust for people. He fears that he is not as significant as he would like to believe. He fears that he is not as independent as he would like to believe. And he greatly fears being controlled by other people. To him, being vulnerable to someone is being controlled. He is afraid that his vulnera-bility will be used against him, so he resists close-ness even though, in many cases, he truly desires it. He cannot imagine divulging his future, feelings, thoughts, and goals to another person. Even

> though his fears are misguided, it is very difficult to
> convince him otherwise. The only person he ends
> up trusting is himself.[8]

Dr. Field blames the problem of low self-esteem on parents for expecting too much from their children, making them seem worthless or inept. Such ideas spawned early can often extend into adulthood. In disciplining children, parents should make clear that they object not to the *total child* but to a specific objectionable behavior for which correction must be administered. A parent may cause irreparable harm when he grabs his head and moans, "Johnnie, what am I going to do with you? Can't you ever do anything right?" What child is going to argue with his parent? If Dad considers him a klutz, then he will remain a klutz into adulthood—particularly if he is a Melancholy. Unreasonable demands on children during their ripening years can be devastating to their self-image. Field warns, "Even when he is an adult, this can have a definite negative effect on his marriage."[9]

> When I suspect this problem, I ask a person to tell
> me what he likes about himself. He is usually very
> uncomfortable; it would be much simpler if he
> could tell me what he does *not* like. His worth and
> value are not based upon internal personal worth,
> but on his external performance. He may actually
> be very successful in business or sports, but it isn't
> enough. He feels he has to be perfect to make up
> for his internally-felt shortcomings.

> A woman with low self-image often approaches marriage on the basis of what she can get rather than on
> what she wants. She doesn't believe she can commandeer the individual who will fulfill her dreams,
> so she compromises. After all, if she doesn't feel
> good about herself, why should anyone else? If low
> self-esteem is acute, she may even think she doesn't

deserve to be happy or successful. Then she may find
it extremely uncomfortable to let other people love
her because she doesn't love herself.[10]

A classic example of this occurred in a Southern city.
Seated across from me was an absolutely beautiful
"Southern belle" in her mid-forties. After a little chitchat
she softly asked, "Can you tell me why I am becoming so
suspicious of my husband?" She had been married to the
handsome hulk sitting next to her for 25 years and loved
him very much. Typically (as she described him) he was
busy talking to the woman on the other side of him. Then
she offered this tidbit: "My husband claims he has never
been unfaithful to me, but he is very attractive to the opposite sex, and I am afraid some woman will steal him." I
naively asked what she was doing about it. With a slight
blush she replied, "I seduce him every morning before he
goes to work."

With as straight a face as I could muster, I inquired
about his response. She frowned and murmured, "That's
what bothers me. He's beginning to avoid me, which only
underscores my fears that he may have found someone
else." Estimating his age as close to 50, I advised, "That may
not be the problem at all. Lovemaking is exciting for a man
his age, but six or seven days a week is a little much even for
the most virile." Believe it or not, she had never considered
that! Of course not. She was too self-centered to think of
him. Her seductive role, which most husbands would welcome two or three times a week, was inspired not by agape
love but by self-love.

## Selfishness Equals Lack of Love

The "Southern belle" assuredly loved her husband, but
not as much as she loved herself. She adored being known
as his wife, showing off his good looks, and being treated
"as a perfect lady." Unfortunately, she wanted him for the

wrong reasons. He existed as a spouse to fulfill her life. His needs came second or third—or not at all.

The Bible says, "Let nothing be done through selfish ambition or conceit, but in lowliness of mind let each esteem others better than himself. Let each of you look out not only for his own interests, but also for the interests of others" (Philippians 2:3,4). True love is a giving, doing, sharing emotion that seeks primarily to benefit another person, not accrue gains for itself. One reason I enjoy Christmas so much is that I get to watch my married children choose gifts for their partners. Although two of them are in Christian work and live on very limited budgets, they express their love each year by scrimping and saving for months before the holiday in order to bestow a gift rich in love. An object that brings pleasure is worth any cost. Love simply cannot wait to give.

The lower part of the diagram on page 139 is based on the most magnificent description of love in the world, 1 Corinthians 13:4-7. Note these words and examine the contrast to selfishness.

## Love and Selfishness Contrasted

I have witnessed self-inflicted pain in thousands of counselees. An experienced divorce judge told me that most of the people to whom he granted divorces could have avoided marital discord if they were not so selfish. Remember, self-centeredness is an attitude of mind; and like love, it is an emotion. Neither can be seen, but both are demonstrated by our actions. The diagram on page 141 is self-explanatory.

## How to Overcome Selfishness

Self-indulgence can be overcome and replaced by love—but only with God's help. Quite honestly, I do not know how to subdue it without His power. It is so difficult

| Characteristics of Selfishness | Characteristics of Love |
|:---:|:---:|
| Impatient | Patient |
| Unkind | Kind |
| Proud | Sincere |
| Stingy | Generous |
| Suspicious | Humble |
| Self-Seeking | Polite |
| Inconsiderate | Trusting |
| Demanding | Gracious |
| | Unselfish |

Diagram 3: Characteristics of Selfishness and Love

to control that restraint or mastery is never automatic, even for Christians. The following steps to conquering this lifetime problem work for those who know Christ and are willing to seek Him, His Spirit, and His Word for victory. If you need them, work carefully on this section. Memorize each step and use it daily. I have used this approach successfully in the counseling room many times.

*1. Face and confess every selfish thought or deed as sin!*

> If we confess our sins, He is faithful and just to forgive us our sins and to cleanse us from all unrighteousness (1 John 1:9).

This first step is like a giant hurdle; it must be taken or we will never finish the race. The person who excuses or tries to justify his selfishness will forever be its slave.

Selfishness
Anger
Criticism
Fear
Worry    =
Immorality
Conflicting roles
Deception
Rebellion

Diagram 4: Lack of Love

Blaming selfishness on temperament or on being raised as an only child will not work. Like any other sin-habit, selfishness must be faced realistically as a sin.

*2. Prayerfully ask God to remove this dreadful habit and fill you with His Holy Spirit.*

> This is the confidence that we have in Him, that if we ask anything according to His will, He hears us. And if we know that He hears us, whatever we ask, we know that we have the petitions that we have asked of Him (1 John 5:14,15).

This verse guarantees that whenever we petition God for something within His specific will, He will do it! We know it is God's will that we overcome our natural bent toward selfishness. Therefore, when we sincerely ask Him to stifle this habit pattern, we can be sure that He will.

Selfishness is an attitude of life that becomes a lifetime habit, and in some people a compulsion. It can be broken, but not without effort. As the above verse teaches, if we ask God to execute His will in our lives, we can be confident that He will do so. The Bible is clear: God definitely intends us to overcome the lifetime habit of selfishness. But just asking one time will not quell such an entrenched mental attitude. Persist in asking Him to take it away after each confession. Gradually the love of the Holy Spirit and the faithful study of His Word will overcome it.

*3. Replace selfish actions with generous service to others.*

> ... submitting to one another in the fear of God
> (Ephesians 5:21).

One evidence of the Spirit-filled life is a submissive spirit. Selfishness is self-seeking, whereas a person with a submissive spirit will seek to serve others. Whenever possible, try to replace every selfish thought or action by thoughtful, generous conduct, directing your attitude outward rather than inward.

*4. Practice giving generously.*

> When you do a charitable deed, do not let your left
> hand know what your right hand is doing, that your
> charitable deed may be in secret; and your Father
> who sees in secret will Himself reward you openly
> (Matthew 6:3,4).

Selfish people always have a problem in giving, whether to God or to man. Start by tithing to your local church, then invest as you are able to other ministries worthy of your support. Not only will God bless you finan-cially, as He has promised to those who honor Him with "their firstfruits," but you will find it increasingly easier to contribute to other people.

One selfish man I counseled still owned a train set from his childhood. After being convicted by God of his selfish-ness, he discovered a boy in a poor home who had repeat-edly requested a minimal train set. I don't know who enjoyed the experience more when that old, unused train traded owners, he or the boy with the "new train." Not long after that my friend called and asked if I knew of a family that needed a car. He had decided that his immaculate trade-in might be appreciated by a needy family. Obviously he was getting the message. A short time later his wife came to me between church services. "I don't know what you did to my husband, but he is a different man!" I had simply challenged him to be a giver instead of a taker. He accepted the challenge, and today he and his wife have found, as our Lord promised, that "it is better to give than to receive."

*5. Give love to your partner and family each day.*

> Above all these things put on love, which is the
> bond of perfection (Colossians 3:14).

The cure for selfishness is not complete until you have learned to express love. Keep in mind that just as selfishness produces added selfishness, so love begets love. Determine that with God's help you will become a giver, beginning with your own family. Fill your home with compliments, courte-sies, gifts, and kindnesses unlimited. It will enrich your own life and create an aura of love that will penetrate every corner of your home.

*6. Memorize Philippians 2:3,4 and incorporate it into your lifestyle.*

> Let nothing be done through selfish ambition or
> conceit, but in lowliness of mind let each esteem
> others better than himself. Let each of you look out
> not only for his own interests, but also for the
> interests of others.

The psalmist challenges us to hide God's Word in our heart so we do not sin against Him. Selfish people sin because of an egocentric mental attitude. Replace that with the one the Holy Spirit admonishes us to maintain in Philippians 2:3,4. Memorizing this verse of Scripture and repeating it daily in prayer will help to establish an "others-consciousness," displacing your old habit pattern.

### 7. *Give yourself to God to help others.*

> Likewise you also, reckon yourselves to be dead
> indeed to sin, but alive to God in Christ Jesus our
> Lord. Therefore do not let sin reign in your mortal
> body, that you should obey it in its lusts. And do not
> present your members as instruments of unright-
> eousness to sin, but present yourselves to God as
> being alive from the dead, and your members as
> instruments of righteousness to God (Romans 6:11-
> 13).

The happiest individuals in the world are people-helpers. The most miserable are the selfish. Dedicate yourself to serving the living creatures He loves most—mankind. Not only will you please God by such pursuits, but you will sustain other people as well, and in the process gain a sense of fulfillment unobtainable at any other level.

### 8. *Practice being kind to those you meet.*

> Be kind to one another, tenderhearted, forgiving
> one another, even as God in Christ forgave you
> (Ephesians 4:32).

People are starved for kindness today. Go out of your way to be considerate—and start in your home. At first you may have to practice this response consciously when meeting others, but with God's help you can develop it into a lifestyle. The spirit of friendship always generates a friendly smile, a warm embrace, and kindly deeds.

*9. Read the Word daily!*

All Christians benefit from a consistent daily reading of the Word of God. We all need to think God's thoughts, and that only comes by filling our mind with His word, which reveals His perspective. Pick up an inexpensive spiral notebook about the size of your Bible and keep a daily journal, entering at least one special thought you receive from the Word each day. Then occasionally review these thoughts, for they will enrich your mind. Plan to read one to five chapters each day, at least five days a week.

## Summary

Replacing a lifetime habit pattern is not easy; it takes time. And don't be surprised if two victories are followed by a defeat. But every time you recognize the old self-indulgent habits creeping back into your lifestyle, reapply these steps to victory over selfishness. With God's help they will change your life!

# *Giant Step Two: The Cause and Cure of Incompatibility*

A woman whose marriage ceremony I had performed 22 years earlier, now the mother of five sons, came in for counseling and almost immediately announced, "Bob and I are thinking about getting a divorce. We are incompatible." Then she added, "I just can't stand to have him touch me!"

I almost laughed out loud. As she spoke, my mind rushed back to a Sunday evening church service 22 years before our encounter when they were so "compatible" that I had to send an usher to the back row of the church to sit between them. They simply couldn't keep their hands off each other! Yet 22 years and five children later, she cringed at the thought of personal contact.

That experience taught me that incompatibility is a learned behavior. If a pair of lovebirds, whose every touch sends emotional shockwaves coursing through them, can learn to become incompatible, why can't untouchables with God's help learn to become compatible again?

The natural drive toward the opposite sex is so powerful that a clear reason must exist when two former compatibles are turned off toward each other. The usual turnoff (after selfishness) results from the clash of two predominant emotions—anger and fear. If those two opposition forces collide often enough, even the greatest lovers will become incompatible.

## Angry Types Attract Fearful Types

The contrasting temperaments that most strongly attract each other (Sanguines to Melancholies and Cholerics to Phlegmatics) bring to marriage contrasting negative emotions. Sanguines and Cholerics suffer from an anger problem; the other two are predominantly fearful. Consequently, a person who is prone to anger tends to marry one who is subject to fear, and vice versa. The clashing of these two emotions will ultimately destroy their love and cause them to become incompatible.

When two very well-matched young people marry, their newfound love will drive their natural anger and fear into the background. For a time after the wedding, the act of marriage is so exciting that feelings of love usually run off the charts. But after the honeymoon, when they return to the real world of decisions and revisions, pressures begin to mount. And sooner or later IT happens—the couple's first real explosion, triggered by a clash of wills or the angry expressions of one partner. As soon as the incensed mate explodes, the fearful partner pulls back into his shell of self-protection, creating a chasm between them. This, of course, is not fatal; they have merely experienced their first "lover's quarrel."

"Making up" usually follows, and the couple reunites in love—but now with a difference. Their first explosion has created a thin layer of scar tissue. They have taught each other a lesson: "If you push me too far, I will explode!" "If you explode, I will withdraw into my shell—or run home to Mama." After reconciliation, love can still penetrate that scar tissue, but when one conflagration is followed by another, cruel words will lacerate and tear, and the fearful temperament will retreat again into his protective shell. A cycle of "making up" followed by angry outbursts and fearful withdrawals will form a scar tissue between them so thick that love will either die or become too weak to penetrate it. Incompatibility becomes inevitable.

At this point the individuals are no longer looking through the rose-colored glasses of love but begin to view each other objectively—or negatively. The fearful person tries to shield himself by withdrawal and/or criticism of his partner mentally or verbally; the angry spouse's frustration level increases, and more explosions follow. Sexual coldness between them only compounds the problem.

It is important to understand here that angry temperaments are not always men, though irate males are usually more violent and noisy in the expression of hostile feelings than angry women. In the case of the incompatible couple mentioned above, it was the woman who became angry. Bob was an easygoing, hardworking, dependable introvert who fell silent when his wife exploded. "I just don't know what to do or say when she gets like that!" he declared. She would detonate again because of his passivity.

In the long run both anger and fear are more powerful than love. The Bible tells a husband to love his wife and not be bitter against her. Why? Because bitterness nullifies love. According to the Bible, "The fear of man brings a snare," but "perfect love casts out fear." I have counseled women who were so fearful about being hurt when they made love that their normal body functions closed down and they could not consummate the act of marriage. In the case of men, sometimes the fear of nonperformance or premature ejaculation actually causes it to happen.

Love is a natural emotion. A normal, healthy person will love other people unless impeded by anger or fear. I once watched the water in an Arizona irrigation canal flowing freely for miles until it suddenly encountered a dam. Then it abruptly stopped. Love and compatibility are like that—flowing naturally unless they are dammed up by anger or fear.

These two emotions are not simply the result of a person's temperament. Background, childhood training, and spiritual motivation will also determine their dominance. A fear-prone Phleg-Mel brought up in a loving Christian home will have much less of a problem with fear than one raised in a cruel or molesting environment. The same holds true for an anger-prone person who lived in a consistent Christian home that refused to permit the child to indulge his or her hot temper at will. He will proceed into marriage fully able to control his natural emotions. For this reason couples should date long enough before marriage to anticipate each other's emotional reactions. However, just knowing the potential for negative emotional expression is not enough. Sometimes it takes marriage to reveal what a person really is.

## Anger and Fear: Primary Emotions

All human beings possess a variety of emotions, but chief among them is either anger or fear. So prominent are these two emotions that by the time I had counseled more than 1500 people, I remarked to my wife, "Everyone who comes for counseling is either angry or fearful. The only exceptions are those with both problems." Now that I have counseled another 4500 individuals, that observation has been confirmed. Depending, of course, on background and childhood training, these two problems tend to haunt people throughout their lives, including their marriage. The following diagram will illustrate which temperaments gravitate to which problem.

Temperament combinations represent a person's predisposition toward these emotional problems. Besides childhood training and spiritual maturity, the result of habit must be considered. Any anger-prone young person who has seen adults display resentment and rage during his

# Temperament-Induced Emotional Problems

• • •

| ANGER | FEAR | ANGER/FEAR |
|---|---|---|
| Chlor-San | Phleg-Mel | San-Mel |
| San-Chlor | Mel-Phleg | San-Phleg |
| Chlor-Mel | Phleg-San | Mel-Chlor |
| Chlor-Phleg | | Mel-San |
| | | Phleg-Chlor |

• • •

Diagram 5: Temperament-Induced Emotional Problems

impressionable years will develop a strong habit of exploding into anger when he is crossed. Each time he will become a little more entrenched in that habit pattern. But the initial tendency to react with anger or fear is largely the result of a person's inherited temperament.

People have often asked me how I became so enamored with temperament theory in the first place. Shortly after I discovered that people who came to my counseling room had either an anger or fear problem (or both), a minister friend gave me a copy of O. Hallesby's book, *Temperament and the Christian Faith,* which offers a detailed description of the four temperaments. When I read that book, for the first time I understood why people reflected one or the other of these problems. As we have seen, Sanguines and Cholerics have a natural predisposition to anger, Melancholies and Phlegmatics to fear.

During that same period of time, I had discovered that the Spirit-filled life was the remedy for overcoming human weaknesses. Consequently, I applied that teaching to the overcoming of temperament-induced weaknesses. In fact, the working title for my first book, believe it or not, was *How to Overcome Your Weaknesses by the Filling of the Holy Spirit.* Just before I sent it to the printer (I was so internationally unknown then that I was obligated to print it myself), my daughter Linda admonished, "Dad, you can't give your book such a long title." And she was right. After much discussion she came up with the suggestion *Spirit-Controlled Temperament.* Needless to say, that book changed my life. And from comments I have received, God has used it in the lives of many of the over one million people who have read it.

All that occurred 32 years and over 4000 counseling encounters ago. Today I am more convinced than ever that most people have by nature a predisposition toward anger or fear due primarily to temperament. Interestingly enough, the cure for both is identical. Therefore I will describe each in detail and save the cure for the end of this chapter.

## Why Anger Is a Harmful Emotion

At the outset we need to distinguish between righteous indignation and the kind of personal anger I am addressing here. The Bible makes allowance for the former. Ephesians 4:26,27 tells us, " 'Be angry and do not sin:' do not let the sun go down on your wrath, nor give place to the devil." Obviously there is a place for such indignation. The difference between the personal anger which the Bible condemns and righteous indignation is that the first is selfish. When we become righteously indignant over someone or something besides ourselves, we are opposing a principle or practice of injustice.

Our Lord was righteously indignant when He drove the money-changers out of the temple for defaming His Father's house. But He did not become angry when they buffeted Him, crowned Him with thorns, or crucified Him. That would have been personal, selfish, and sinful, whereas He was without sin. The Christian who looks at the catastrophic abortion rate, pornography, licensed perversion, and other signs of moral degeneracy in our society without feeling righteous indignation has no moral backbone. The Bible tells us that God hates sin; this is righteous (or sinless) indignation at the principle of moral evil. The kind of anger that the Bible condemns is based on *selfishness* and is aimed at an individual, not a principle.

The following six reasons explain why indulging in anger at a person is wrong.

### 1. *The Bible calls anger sin!*

In the Sermon on the Mount (considered by many to be the most beautiful teaching in all literature), our Lord said:

> You have heard that it was said to those of old, "You shall not murder," and whoever murders will be in danger of the judgment. But I say to you that whoever is angry with his brother without a cause shall be in danger of the judgment (Matthew 5:21,22).

The seriousness of the sin of anger appears in this text, for our Lord put it on a par with murder. In the eyes of God, a person who hates another, even for a short time, is guilty of murdering that individual. No wonder such an emotion destroys love! I live in the murder capital of the world, Washington D.C., where more murders are performed per capita than in any other city. It is an intensely angry city. Domestic violence, gang wars, child abuse, political assassinations, street crimes—they abound in our nation's capital. Anger leads to murder, and that is why God condemns it.

Many Scriptures denounce anger. If you look up the word "anger" in a Bible concordance, you will be amazed at its frequency. Proverbs 29:22 says it all: "An angry man [or woman] stirs up strife, and a furious man abounds in transgression." Anger is a motivational emotion that creates havoc and incites other sins, at home or in the workplace.

## 2. Anger impairs our judgment.

A professional football star became so angry at his coach during a team meeting that he lashed out at him in front of the other players. The coach became so enraged in turn that he kicked the player out of the meeting, bellowing, "You will never play for me again." The rift was so bad between the two that the player had to be traded, which cost both the team and the player dearly. The player was sent to a second-rate team as quarterback, and his original team failed to make the playoffs that year for lack of a good quarterback.

Similar behavior occurs between married couples and family members, destroying relationships. In many such cases only the grace and power of God can heal them. Many divorced couples have lived to regret the anger that ruined their union.

## 3. Anger provokes hurtful speech.

The shortest nerve in the body is the one between the emotional center and the tongue. Your emotional center, lodged between your temples and behind your forehead, is walnut-shaped and serves as the emotional computer of your body, for it is neurologically tied to every organ in your body. Next to those that go to your eyelids, the shortest nerve goes to your most powerful organ for helping or hurting people—your tongue. When motivated by anger, the tongue is always destructive. Meant by God to communicate edification or helpful words of love, that member when used in anger strips those we love of self-respect and causes partners to indulge their weakness—fear.

Colossians 3:8,9 calls us to put off three hostile emotions, which create three harmful speech patterns:

> You must also put off all these: *anger, wrath, malice,* blasphemy, filthy language out of your mouth. Do not lie to one another, since you have put off the old man with his deeds (emphasis added).

The diagram on the next page should be very enlightening.

Why do people "blaspheme" (meaning slander) God or man? Because they love Him so? Certainly not. They are angry. Why do people say filthy things about the opposite sex? Because they think so well of them? Hardly. In most cases, they have never developed a viable relationship with a member of the opposite sex in their entire life; consequently they speak disparagingly. And when angry, even those who are generally truthful will lie. According to Proverbs 26:28, "A lying tongue hates those it hurts" (NIV). In other words, lies that injure others are motivated by anger. It's an old story: Rejection leads to anger, anger destroys good emotions, and the result is slanderous, filthy, or lying speech.

Any divorce judge will tell you that by the time angry couples reach his courtroom, they have devastated each other with their mouths—which demolishes even the most vibrant relationships, often permanently.

*4. Anger destroys your health.*

Most people have no idea what a powerful influence emotions have over their physical well-being. The killing diseases—heart attack, high blood pressure, stroke, etc.— are much more potent among people with anger and fear problems. When a person says, "I can't stomach him," he is

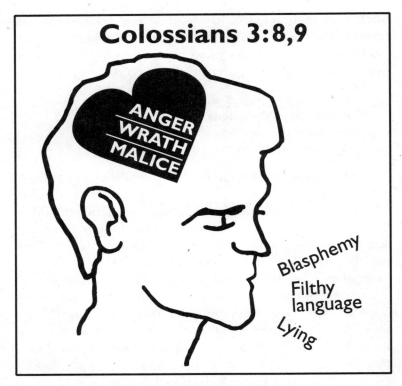

Diagram 6: Verbal Results of Anger

right. The lining of his stomach wall cannot withstand the high acid content generated by anger, thus giving him bleeding ulcers. In Columbus, Ohio, a doctor who described himself as an ulcer specialist took issue with my quote from Dr. Henry Brandt that "97 percent of the people I have counseled because of bleeding ulcers had them because they were angry." The specialist urged, "I think it is more like 100 percent!" I'll let the two experts battle it out for the 3 percent difference.

The point is this: The man you start hating can ruin your health. Dr. S.I. McMillen in his excellent book *None of*

*These Diseases* lists 51 maladies that people can bring on themselves unnecessarily due to protracted anger, including ulcers, heart attack, high blood pressure, colitis, kidney stones, and gallbladder ailments.

One of the tragic cases I recall is of a man whom I confronted with his anger in a restaurant over lunch. He mildly replied, "LaHaye, that's the way I am! I'm a striker. In the Navy it helped me work my way up from a 17-year-old kid to the highest enlisted rank the Navy has. Now that I'm retired and have gone into insurance sales, my goal is to reach the million-dollar round table my first year." Obviously I was dealing with a Chlor-Mel with a strong hostility problem that he refused to face. When I warned him that he would destroy his family (which was the purpose of our meeting), he retorted, "LaHaye, that's your job. You tell my family to shape up or ship out!" When I cautioned that his physical body couldn't stand that kind of stress indefinitely, he laughed. "That's where I've really got you. I had a complete physical exam two weeks ago, and the doctors tell me I'm in perfect health."

Little did either of us realize that seven months later, when he erupted in anger at the office over the mistake of a secretary who forgot one zero on an insurance contract (reducing it from $2.5 million to $250,000), his face turned beet red and he burst a blood vessel in his head, spilling blood out onto his brain. For the next 12 years he sat like a mindless child, staring all day at television. In a single angry moment he was reduced from one of the sharpest people I knew to an unemployable incompetent.

In all fairness, he probably had a congenital weakness in that blood vessel that would have perforated sooner or later, but I am confident that his anger burst the vessel long before it was necessary. Anger is a destructive emotion that can ruin one's health and destroy normal bodily functions. If you have any doubts, please read *None of These Diseases*. Anger that produces long-term resentment can create

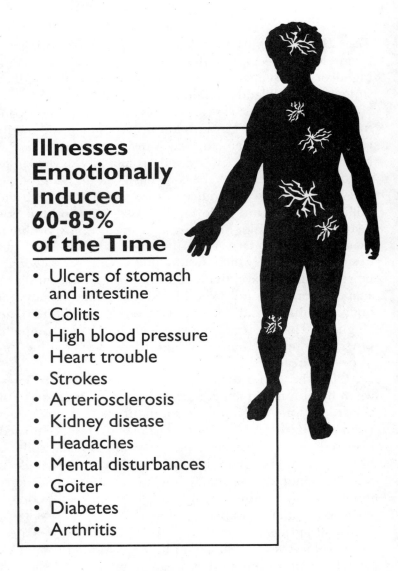

# Illnesses Emotionally Induced 60-85% of the Time

- Ulcers of stomach and intestine
- Colitis
- High blood pressure
- Heart trouble
- Strokes
- Arteriosclerosis
- Kidney disease
- Headaches
- Mental disturbances
- Goiter
- Diabetes
- Arthritis

Diagram 7: Illnesses Emotionally Induced

sexual dysfunction in otherwise perfectly healthy people—
frigidity in women and impotence in men.

## 5. *Anger grieves the Holy Spirit.*

God wants all Christians to walk in the Spirit, meaning
to live in the control of the Spirit. In our next chapter we
will explain what this means, but suffice it to say here that
a Spirit-controlled life is impossible for an angry Christian. Nothing except selfishness will destroy a Christian's
spiritual existence like anger. Just examine Ephesians
4:30-32:

> Do not grieve the Holy Spirit of God, by whom you
> were sealed for the day of redemption. Let all bit-
> terness, wrath, anger, clamor, and evil speaking be
> put away from you, with all malice. And be kind to
> one another, tenderhearted, forgiving one another,
> just as God in Christ also forgave you.

Grieving the Spirit in that context is done by permitting
one's self to indulge five hostile emotions and one harmful
speech pattern. Note the outlawed emotions that grieve the
Spirit: 1) "bitterness"—people harbor bitterness because of
insults, but this text teaches forgiveness; 2) "wrath"—a
long-term burn; 3) "anger"—internal feelings that erupt;
4) "clamor"—loud shouting, crying, or speaking; 5) "evil
speaking"—"I hate you," "I wish we had never married";
6) "malice"—"enmity of heart," a hatred so strong that it
impels one to injure. These angry feelings that culminate
long-term evil thinking parallel our Lord's comparison of
anger to murder, which puts one in danger of "hell fire."
We cannot set our minds on positive things (Philippians
4:8) or "things above" and on anger at the same time. One
or the other will dominate. Unless dealt with properly as
sin, angry thoughts will prevail—until we stop grieving the
Holy Spirit in our minds.

The most condemnatory passage of Scripture on habitual anger is Proverbs 22:24,25:

> Make no friendship with an angry man, and with a furious man do not go, lest you learn his ways and set a snare for your soul.

Note the two results of close contact with an angry person: 1) he is contagious; and 2) he sets a "snare for your soul." No Christian will ever measure up to his potential for Christ who does not let the Spirit of God conquer his anger. Moses is a perfect example. During a lifetime battle with anger, he once became so enraged that he slammed the freshly made Ten Commandments to the ground and broke them. God forgave him and used him after that, but he finally crossed the line. When God told him to "speak to the rock" in order to induce water from it, he became so enraged at the people that he struck the rock with his rod. God then announced, "That is enough."

Consequently, instead of leading the children of Israel into the Promised Land, Moses was forced to transfer the mantle of leadership to Joshua. The great lawgiver died before his time—because of uncontrolled anger. Many a Christian has shortened his life unnecessarily because of protracted anger, which "grieves the Holy Spirit" and "sets a snare to your soul." In other words, under the emotional impetus of anger, we do things that are displeasing to God and detrimental to our spiritual, physical, and family life.

### 6. Anger destroys your love.

Everyone wants to love and be loved. But the person who enters marriage harboring bitterness toward someone in his background will eventually forfeit love for his spouse, one who is innocent of provoking such anger.

People filled with wrath take a respite from their anger long enough to fall in love, but after marriage, anger returns

with a vengeance. It is an entrenched habit that, with sufficient provocation, will be turned on the love object. And
that triggers the anger-fear syndrome mentioned above,
leading to incompatibility.

Proverbs 10:12 admonishes, "Hatred stirs up strife, but
love covers all sins." That is why the relationship between
angry-fearful partners deteriorates. Each time anger flares
up at the exposure of a partner's weakness, love dies a little.
But note the contrast: "Love covers all sins." At least four
times that statement, which indicates that love is blind to
faults and mistakes, appears in Scripture. First Peter 4:8 is
one of them: "Love will cover a multitude of sins."

Angry individuals are not usually forgiving people, for
they tend to remember insults, affronts, or mistakes for
long periods of time. They desperately need to learn the
biblical art of forgiveness, and their partner will greatly
profit from such a lesson. Ephesians 4:32 commands us to
"be kind to one another, tenderhearted, forgiving one
another, just as God in Christ also forgave you."

A lady stopped me after a seminar and asked, "Can you
tell me why I cannot respond to my husband emotionally?"
I first wondered whether he had mistreated her and was
angry and cruel. But she surprised me by saying, "My husband is the kindest, nicest, most gentle man I have ever
met."

Something was dreadfully wrong! I thought all women
responded to tenderness, but not her. In fact she added,
"Whenever he comes to me for affection, I feel I am being
smothered. I don't even like for him to kiss me." So I asked
the obvious: "Were you molested as a child?" "Yes, in the
fourth grade." "You haven't forgiven the man?" Suddenly a
flood of anger swirled furiously. "Why should I forgive
him?" she raged. "He should be shot for treating defense-
less little girls that way."

I couldn't agree with her more, but I told her, "You will
never learn to respond to your husband normally until you

can forgive that man." It was a man she didn't know and did not see well enough to identify afterward. "But he doesn't deserve such forgiveness," she responded. I agreed. "But that is not the basis on which we are commanded to forgive others. We are to forgive as God in Christ forgave us."

Three years later that woman sought God's help to forgive a degenerate man, and today can enjoy her "kind, nice, gentle husband." Anger destroys, but forgiveness heals and enables us to love as God commanded us.

In most marriages of any length, much forgiveness is needed. Because none of us is perfect, sooner or later we will treat our partner selfishly or cruelly. The moment we refuse to forgive, we start to die. You doubtless remember the adage, "To err is human, to forgive divine." That is quite accurate. We don't need God's help to err, but we do need Him to forgive. One of the best book titles I have ever seen announces *Love or Perish!* Love and the many forms of anger cannot coexist in the human heart. Either you will forgive and go on loving, or your love will perish. And a loveless marriage is often worse than no marriage at all.

Again, you do not have to be dominated by anger, for God has provided a cure which I shall outline at the end of this chapter. First, however, let us consider the other problem that destroys marriage relationships—*fear* in its many forms.

### The Problem of Fear

It should not surprise us that fear is a major problem, because the Bible addresses it so many times. There are 365 "fear nots" in the Bible, one for each day of the year. Our Lord addressed this problem in Matthew 6:25-34 (part of His superlative Sermon on the Mount), actually giving it more space than He did to the subject of anger. In short, He admonished people not to be anxious or worried (forms of fear) about "what you will eat or what you will drink" or what you shall wear, but to trust God for tomorrow. Those who are fearful of the unknown He called "O you of little faith." Obviously faith is the antidote to fear.

Many people are deceived about fear because it does not produce violent outbursts like anger. However, it is just as powerful and destructive, if not to others, certainly to the fearful person himself. Fear is a cruel taskmaster which inhibits every area of one's life. It is the paralyzing emotion that restricts normal feelings of love, confidence, and well-being. It actuates negative thought patterns, thereby breeding anxiety, worry, and the other negative emotions which can grow like a giant snowball until they consume a person's entire life.

Several years ago *Reader's Digest* published an article on fear written by a minister. For ten years he had penned a daily question-and-answer column for a newspaper which was read by one million people. Based on those thousands of questions, he offered the following insightful statement:

> Private enemy number one in human life is neither sin nor sorrow; it is FEAR! The most rife is fear of ourselves, fear of failure, breakdown, and poverty, making life an agony. Next to fear is the nagging, gnawing worry which wears us out and makes us unfit for living. Worry is a tiny rivulet seeping into the mind like slow poison, until it paralyzes us. Unless it is checked, it cuts a channel into which all other thoughts are drained.

This description of fear is painfully accurate. And it does not automatically lessen with age and maturity. Fearsome thoughts become a way of life, and may even shorten that life.

The following chart, used by permission of Dr. Jay Adams, is from his excellent book *Competent to Counsel*. It shows the entire cycle of life activities. Notice the next diagram, which delineates fear, worry, and anxiety at the core of a person's thinking. You can see how it reaches into every

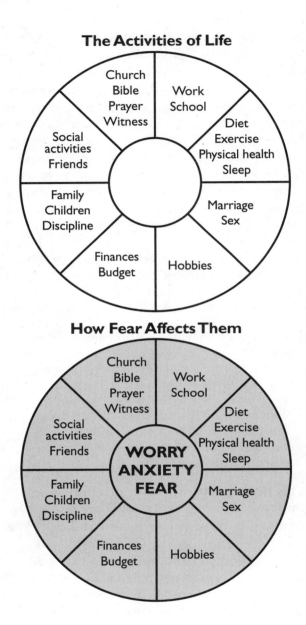

Diagram 8: Activities of Life

area of one's life. Fear is not related only to one facet of life, such as vocation, but to your emotions. Like cancer of the blood, it invades the total being.

Examining the chart on the previous page, you will begin to appreciate the pervasiveness of fear. For example, many bright young people stop their education with high school graduation. When you ask them in their mid-thirties, "Why didn't you attend college?" they will usually respond, "At 19 I was afraid I couldn't cut it," or "I was afraid I couldn't afford it." Now that they have worked with other people, many who did pursue a college degree and some not as bright as they are, they admit that it was not absence of intelligence but lack of confidence.

In the life of a church, many fine people, some of them deeply dedicated to God, never serve Him—not because they are carnal and unconcerned, but because fear over-powers them. That certainly is true of witnessing. Scores of people would love to share their faith with friends and neighbors but never do—not because they are indifferent, but because fear is more powerful than concern. The Bible says, "Whatever is not from faith is sin" (Romans 14:23). That is why you must never let fear keep you from fulfilling God's desires for your life.

Everyone will face fear the first time he does anything dangerous in life; that is not surprising. The trauma of dri-ving a car, piloting an airplane, or diving off a ten-foot plat-form will generate a fearful reaction. But those who let fear inhibit them from entering a new sphere of activity have crossed the line from normal to destructive fear.

## Temperament and Fear

Having acknowledged that everyone experiences fear, worry, and anxiety at points in their life, we must admit that some people have a greater problem with them than others. And the differences can be detected in early child-hood. Watch the children in your next Sunday school or

Vacation Bible School program. If the prospect of getting up before a group frightens them, that may become the most terrifying experience of the year. If singing or giving a speech petrifies them, they are dominated by fear. Some children, especially Sanguines and Cholerics, do not hesitate to perform in public and care little what others think of them. Not so with the Melancholy and the Phlegmatic. Children with these temperaments are afraid to leave Mommy's side; they fear getting hurt or being abandoned. As teens they dread rejection by their peers much more than do Cholerics and Sanguines.

I have pondered a great deal about the differences between the fears of the Melancholy and those of the Phlegmatic. In many ways they are similar fears and breed the same ill effects, but those of the Melancholy seem more intense and have a more inhibiting influence. Phlegmatics will allow fear to suppress their activities, but they seldom get as upset. Melancholies who possess a fear of flying break out in a cold sweat and cannot eat or sleep just thinking about it. The Phlegmatic sets his stubborn jaw and declares, "I don't want to go." He will do anything to avoid fear-producing circumstances.

Vocationally, the Phlegmatic is extremely security-conscious. Whenever an opportunity offers a choice between high pay and security, the Phlegmatic will choose the latter. The Melancholy can hardly make the choice. Both are driven by fear. Melancholies rarely change professions—it's too intimidating! One can persuade Phlegmatics to do something new more easily than Melancholies, but the new venture must offer more security than the present position. I suspect that Melancholies choose a lifetime of academic pursuits because they feel secure there, having spent 18 years or so of their first 23 years in school. (Another reason, admittedly, is because they are highly intelligent and have a natural bent for academics.)

The fears of the Melancholy make him insecure about himself. Somehow, even though the mild-mannered Phlegmatic has a difficult time feeling capable enough to aggressively pursue something he wants or needs, his fear is less intense than that of the Melancholy, who rejects himself and his abilities. Melancholies seem more self-centered than Phlegmatics, thus compounding their fears. Remember, a self-centered person will worry about everything, even his worry. One melancholy woman told me, "I suppose you noticed that I didn't take communion today. It was because after I had confessed all my sins, I was afraid there might be one or two sins I forgot." While we may admire her spiritual sensitivity, we are appalled at her fear of displeasing God. No wonder these people are so sad. *"Anxiety in the heart of man causes depression"* (Proverbs 12:25).

## Why Fear Is a Harmful Emotion

Like its alternative, anger, fear is a very damaging emotion, particularly debilitating to creative people. The following six reasons, though not exhaustive, underscore the seriousness of the problem.

*1. The Bible calls fear sin.*

Romans 14:23 sums up many Scriptures on this subject when it affirms, "Whatever is not from faith is sin." The Bible offers many illustrations of individuals who destroyed their lives because of fear. Remember the 12 spies who went into the Land of Promise? Ten brought back a negative report because they saw giants in the land. Two of the spies, Joshua and Caleb, delivered a positive report, confident that God would deliver the land to them. Unfortunately, three million Jews refused to enter Canaan, so they spent the next 40 years in the desert. All the adults over the age of 21 who participated in that fearful decision would die off. Then the next generation, including Joshua and Caleb—the two faithful men of God—went in to possess the land.

The drastic measures God used to punish the children of Israel for their unbelief ought to impress upon us the destructiveness of fear, especially when it translates into unbelief. God fully understands our fright when we are faced with danger or the unknown. He placed within us a natural human response to danger which at times can save our lives. But God opposes fear that prevents us from doing His will. That kind of fear is sin.

God commended the two spies, Joshua and Caleb, for their faith. They had the same panoramic view of Canaan as the ten fearful spies—a land flowing with milk and honey *and* some nine-foot-tall giants. Ignoring the abundant crops, the ten concluded, "We are grasshoppers in their sight." Fear magnifies difficulties and minimizes resources. Joshua and Caleb saw the giants, but they remembered that God was with them. The ten fearful spies could only envision problems without God.

Many Christians waste 40 years on the back side of the desert because they view everything in life through the eyes of fear—which is seeing life without God. Joshua and Caleb were blessed by God, not because they were better-looking or nicer people, but because they overcame their natural fears through faith.

## 2. Fear puts you in bondage.

Someone has described this negative emotion as "the prison house of fear." The apostle Paul concurred in Romans 8:15: "You did not receive the spirit of bondage again to fear." The bondage of fear inhibits people from doing what is right and proper. Even worse, it can keep them from acting in accordance with God's perfect will.

A doctor was scheduled to take his wife to Europe for a medical convention. As they started to board the plane, his wife's fear of flying gripped her to such a degree that she put both hands on the doorway of the plane and refused to move inside. Ultimately my friend had to leave his wife behind. This woman is a Bible study leader and personal soulwinner, but is obsessed with fear.

Another friend's wife is absolutely petrified of elevators. When they travel, she will only stay in hotels that she can reach by way of the stairs. Needless to say, the fear of both women puts a strain on their relationships because it unnecessarily limits their lifestyle.

Recently a young couple married for three months came in for counseling. Because they had not been able to sexually consummate their marriage, the wife had been carefully examined by a gynecologist and told that she was physically able to experience intercourse. But every time her husband tried to penetrate her, she froze up with fear.

Millions of Christians are immobilized by fear at the prospect of teaching a Sunday school class, praying publicly, or witnessing their faith. Most would love to be able to do so, but fear controls them. Many capable Phlegmatic or Melancholy individuals, spiritually dedicated to God, almost never serve Him—not because they don't love Him, but because fear is more powerful than love.

In the early days of our marriage, my own wife would never teach above the sixth grade. She had been trained during her early teens how to minister to children, so she felt comfortable with them, but was terrified at the thought of teaching adults. And that was only one of her fears. Due to a near-drowning experience in childhood, she was absolutely paranoid about water. "Opposites attract each other," of course, so she married a man who was a member of the swimming team in both high school and college. When we moved to San Diego, the water sport capital of the world, I taught all four of our kids to be expert water skiers—but Bev refused to try. She did venture out enough to learn to drive the boat, but water sports never topped her list of pleasant experiences.

Her fears put a crimp in our marriage and often triggered my anger, which only intensified her fear. At times we even haggled over the entertainment of guests in our home. I wished to invite committees, officers, or church groups over for coffee, and though she enjoyed people, she feared how they would judge her housekeeping ability. If I wanted to have a group over, she would always offer 49 excuses—most of them related to cleaning the house from top to bottom. At times I would just invite people and then inform her that they were coming. As you can imagine, that did little for our marriage. After the folks went home, she would admit that she enjoyed entertaining—but that made no difference in her response the next time. As the Bible says, "Fear is bondage"—a bondage that will keep many Christians from receiving a full reward in heaven and may prevent their marriage from being a "heaven-on-earth" experience in this life.

### 3. Fear inhibits communication.

Anyone who has ever sat in a speech class realizes that some people are petrified when it comes to group presentations but that those who are fearfully tongue-tied usually have the most to say. Everyone experiences nervousness at the outset of such a class, but the fearful never make an adjustment.

In a counseling situation, I have found both men and women too fearful to share their innermost secrets with their mate, or even disclose how they really feel about important matters. It's not that they lack strong feelings; fear keeps them from sharing what is really in their heart. Often in the comfort zone of a counselor's office, they will open up for the first time because fear is removed by the presence of a third person. One woman admitted that she had never told her husband she loved him because she was afraid he would take her for granted and become interested in someone else.

Fear, like anger, is based on selfishness and should have no place in a Christian couple's relationship.

### 4. Fear destroys your health.

The destructive forces on the human body due to fear can scarcely be overestimated. Fear is as dangerous as protracted anger, for both put undue tension on the human body and can cause disease or contribute to the collapse of vital organs, plunging the fear-prone individual into a debilitating illness.

I once knew an administrator in a public school who was a very gifted Mel-Phleg. His wife told me he could sit in an easy chair and start worrying about having a heart attack until his heart began to race, and he would proceed through all the physiological symptoms of such an attack. The doctors assured her, "It's all in his head. His heart is perfectly healthy." Eventually he died of a heart attack—in his easy chair, thinking about having one.

Scores of illustrations could be given of Christians who have destroyed their health unnecessarily by fear. One person confided, "I just can't bring myself to think about the future. If I do, I will become so upset that it will make me ill." Such fear does not factor God into the equation. Fear looks at the realities of life and promptly forgets God. I will admit that perilous times will exist just prior to the coming of Christ (2 Timothy 3:1-5), but they should not cause us to fear. Our Lord Himself said, "When you hear of wars and rumors of wars, see that you are not troubled!" In other words, trust *Him,* not the expected outcome of life's precarious circumstances.

I have found a magnificent antidote to fear, repeated seven times in the Word of God. Consider this well:

> Be strong and of good courage, do not fear nor be
> afraid of them; for the Lord your God, He is the
> One who goes with you. He will not leave you nor
> forsake you (Deuteronomy 31:6).

God gave that promise first to Moses, then to the children of Israel. He extended it to Joshua and four other individuals in the Old Testament. Essentially God commanded, "Go . . . and I will be with you." Two thousand years later our Lord came on the scene and delivered the Great Commission to go into all the world and preach the gospel. He added, "And lo, I am with you always, even to the end of the age!"

God's message to all Christians of every age is the same: "Go and I will be with you." If He is present, why should we fear anything?

### 5. Fear quenches the Holy Spirit.

Just as anger grieves the Spirit and keeps the Christian from walking in the Spirit, so fear "quenches" or stifles the Spirit (1 Thessalonians 5:19). Anytime the Christian is used by God, the Holy Spirit works through him. But fear "quenches the Spirit" and keeps the believer from being the kind of person God wants him to be. Many of the fear-prone members of our churches would like to sing in the choir or teach a Sunday school class or share their faith. Yet they never do these things, not due to worldliness, but because they quench the Spirit by their fears.

### 6. Fear destroys your love.

You cannot lastingly love someone whom you fear. You have probably known individuals who feared their parents, which eventually destroyed the love relationship. When such individuals grow to adulthood, they seldom have much affection for their parents. By contrast, the more we love God, the less we fear Him. That must have been what the apostle John meant when he said, "Perfect love casts out fear."

The same is true of marriage. If you fear your partner, it will eventually kill your love. This does not mean that a 100-pound woman should not have a healthy appreciation for her 250-pound husband's strength as superior to hers. But it does suggest that if she fears that he will be cruel or unfaithful, her love will diminish and eventually disappear.

Now do you understand what I mean by saying that anger and fear cause incompatibility? How can a married couple maintain warm feelings for each other when one is given to angry outbursts that create stifling fear in the other? The more fear one manifests, the greater the anger of the other, thus compounding the problem. It is a vicious circle that eventually destroys positive, love-centered feelings.

That is the bad news. Now for the good news: The cycle can be broken! With God's help, both anger and fear can be overcome.

## How to Overcome Anger and Fear

Through years of trying to help people at over 700 seminars and in the counseling room, I have developed a simple formula for overcoming both anger and fear. I know it works because 1)it is thoroughly biblical, 2)many have testified that they tried it and it worked, and 3)my wife and I have watched it change our lives—she from fear and me from anger.

Memorize this simple formula and let it lead you to a whole new way of life.

*1. Face your anger or fear as sin* (Ephesians 4:30-32; Romans 14:23).

The giant step to victory over any sin is to acknowledge it as sin. As long as you justify anger or fear, you will remain its slave. Once I took a Bible teacher to lunch and gently advised him that his angry outburst in class the Sunday before was unacceptable behavior. He retorted, "Pastor, that is just the way I am. I was born a German Choleric, and sometimes I get mad and blow up." Eventually we removed that man from his class, and I watched him drive five children away from his home in anger at both himself and God, torture his wife for years, and die a premature death needlessly—all because he refused to face his anger as sin.

A doctor confided to me at a local hospital, "Preacher, this woman is destroying her body because of her compulsive fears. You can help her better than I can." So I tried to confront her kindly with her lifetime pattern of worry, anxiety, and fear, which was destroying her body, marriage, and spiritual life. I reminded her that God wanted her to "cast all [her] care on Him, for He cares for [her]." But she would have none of it. Instead she indignantly responded, "Someone has to worry about these things!" And she did— experiencing a painful, costly, and unnecessarily early grave.

It is better to face anger and fear, then accept God's label of them: *sin.*

### 2. Confess your anger or fear as sin.

Once you have faced the problem, you are only moments away from God's forgiveness through confession. First John 1:9 makes it clear that whatever the sin in your life, if you confess it in the Savior's name, God will forgive it.

### 3. Ask God to take away your habit pattern of fear or anger.

Because of the power of God within you as a Christian, you are not a slave to habit like unsaved people. A *victim* of habit, yes, but not a slave. With God's help you can extricate yourself from a lifetime of such crippling emotions. First John 5:14,15 promises that whenever you ask God for anything within His will, He will do it! Since we know He is eager for us to gain victory over both anger and fear, we can be confident that He will enable us to break the habit, no matter how entrenched it is.

### 4. Ask for the filling of the Spirit.

Once we have met the conditions of being filled (or "controlled") with the Spirit, all that remains is to ask. Our Lord said, "If you then, being evil, know how to give good gifts to your children, how much more will your heavenly Father give the Holy Spirit to those who ask Him!" (Luke 11:13).

### 5. Forgive the person toward whom you have a grudge or bitterness.

The Bible tells us that "if [we] regard iniquity in [our] heart," the Lord will not hear us when we pray (Psalm 66:18). If there is someone who has rejected, injured, or offended you, forgive him. That is a command of God. Harboring bitterness in one's heart is like cancer—it spreads to the whole person. Remember the lady who was molested? She could not respond normally in love to her husband until she forgave the molester. And so must you if any person is the object of your wrath or bitterness.

### 6. Thank God by faith for the victory over fear or anger.

Faith is the appropriation of God's promises before they become fact. As an act of faith, obey 1 Thessalonians 5:18 and give thanks for your anticipated victory even before it comes. Such thanksgiving is the "will of God."

### 7. Repeat! Repeat! And repeat!

It is unrealistic to expect permanent victory over an evil habit, one that has ruled you for so many years, in one application of this seven-step formula. In fact, I can almost guarantee that although you will enjoy victory for a time, sooner or later you will revert to your old habit pattern. Bad habits usually maintain an incredible hold on our lives. But you can have victory!

At this point many Christians have failed. They listen intently as the adversary of their soul whispers, "See, I told you it wouldn't work; you just blew up again," or, "You just limited God again by fear." Don't pay any attention to him. Immediately repeat the first six steps to this formula—and do so every time you revert to habit. *Gradually* your outbursts of anger or fear will begin to diminish until their stranglehold on you is broken.

The key to success involves immediate recognition of sin and repetition of this formula. Soon you will find yourself "a new person in Christ Jesus." It can change your life and your marriage. It certainly did ours!

# A Personal Confession

"Confession," they say, "is good for the soul." It will also help to illustrate how very effective the cure formula for anger and fear can be. For as you will see, both my wife and I have been there! To be honest, my wife and I did not always enjoy the marvelous relationship we have built (with the Lord's help) through the years.

About 12 years into our marriage, had I been asked to rate our relationship on a scale of zero to 100, I would have given it a 20. My wife more generously would have scored it a 24. However, at no time did we ever consider divorce. That was simply not an option for us, for several reasons. One, we had three small children for whom divorce would have been devastating. Second, I am a minister; it would have ruined my career. Third, neither of us believed in it. Fourth, my wife is a very stubborn Phleg-San woman, and I am a very determined Chlor-San man. She had made a life-time decision and was stubbornly committed to it. I likewise signed on for life and was determined to "tough it out"— and believe me, it got harder and harder.

Then it happened! Bev attended a Sunday school convention at Forest Home Camp, where she went to become a better junior department superintendent. I was somewhat puzzled at her decision, for I considered her the best super-intendent at her level I had ever seen.

At that time Beverly was also "the ideal minister's wife"—almost. She was beautiful, gracious, and very proper; she would never offend anyone. On the other hand, she was so circumscribed by her fears that she would never address adults; she would allow herself to teach only up to the sixth grade. Just one week before leaving for that convention, she had turned down an opportunity to give a devotional message to eight women in one of our mis-sionary circles. "I never speak to adults," she demurred. "My husband is the speaker in our family; ask him." If you are familiar with my wife's work today as president of Con-cerned Women for America, the largest women's organiza-tion in the country, you may have difficulty relating to the fear-dominated woman that Bev was in her late twenties and early thirties.

The devotional speaker at camp that week was Dr. Henry Brandt, to whom I have dedicated this book. We did not know him then, but through the years he has become a dear friend and inspirational example to us both. His messages immediately focused on Bev's greatest prob-lems—fear, worry, and anxiety—negative emotions that keep people from becoming all they should be for God.

After listening to him for two days, she asked for private counseling. There she admitted that her fears clashed with the aggressive ways of her husband (we were extreme oppo-sites). She explained that I liked to entertain groups from the church in our home, but she needed two months' notice to clean the house from top to bottom. And that was only one of our many areas of conflict.

Finally Dr. Brandt asked if she would *really* like to know the nature of her problem. She assured him that she would. "You won't like it; it isn't very pretty." She replied, "Oh, I can take it." Little did she know that he would identify her as "a very selfish young woman!" He added that she lived like a turtle; only when no one was around would she stick her neck out and go anywhere. "What should I do, Dr. Brandt?" she asked. "Throw away that selfish shell of self-protection and abandon yourself to God. Let Him decide what you should or shouldn't do." She thanked him (Bev is always proper), went back to the cabin, and cried for an hour. Finally she rose to her feet, looked at her reflection in the mirror, and experienced a life-changing moment. She declared to her reflection, "Beverly, Dr. Brandt is right. You *are* a selfish woman, always overprotecting yourself." Sinking to her knees and recommitting her life to God, she took the first big step toward a transformed life.

Bev's transformation did not happen overnight. I can remember a phone call two weeks later from Crestline, California, asking her to be the mother-and-daughter banquet speaker "for 100 women!" She almost panicked and responded negatively. Instead, she trusted God and accepted. She worked on her message every day for 2½ months but was so nervous that she took our daughter and another high-school-aged "missionary daughter" (living in our home) with her for moral support. Five women prayed to receive Christ at the end of her message, and Bev has never been the same since! Later she was invited to speak to 175 women, then 300, then women's conferences. Finally, after she had addressed some of my largest Family Life Seminars, in 1979 I had the opportunity to introduce her in the Long Beach Civic Auditorium to over 7000 men and women, where she spoke for 30 minutes and loved it.

Since then, on TV and elsewhere, she has debated some of the leading feminists and liberals in the country, including Norman Lear. She has appeared on behalf of Supreme Court Justice nominees at the request of former President Ronald Reagan and before the Senate Judiciary Committee, where Senator Ted Kennedy, Joe Biden, and former senator

Howard Metzenbaum directed questions at her in an attempt to shake her confidence—to no avail.

What changed a woman who was afraid of her own shadow to an aggressive advocate of traditional values? God the Holy Spirit! It didn't occur overnight, but gradually fear was replaced by divine strength. She is still hesitant on occasions, but she no longer lets fear limit God's use of her life.

You can't imagine how that has changed our relationship. When we have conflict, instead of clamming up, she honestly shares her views. We can now communicate about anything and she is not apprehensive about her husband's explosive nature. In fact, she realizes that if I should respond in anger, that is my problem. Her job is to do what the Bible says: "Speak the truth in love." Silence is not golden in a marriage relationship; it rarely settles anything, at least when it prevents the utterance of a gently voiced truth.

I have watched a beautiful, tightly bound rosebud blossom before my eyes into an even more beautiful full-blown rose. Week by week, month by month, and finally year by year, she opened herself to God's unfolding will. As she often says, "God leads us from step of faith to step of faith." She has journeyed from junior department superintendent to a well-recognized women's speaker, a college registrar, an author of nine books, a TV co-host with me, founder and chairman of Concerned Women for America, a confidante to two presidents of the United States and the President of Nicaragua, a member of the board of trustees of Liberty University—the largest Christian college in the country—and host of her own daily, half-hour radio call-in talkshow from Washington D.C. with a listening audience of one million.

She has even overcome one of the most powerful of all fear complexes, fear of water. Today my wife swims, as the result of a challenge written by a missionary: "If your wife is really filled with the Holy Spirit, as you said in your book *Spirit-Controlled Temperament,* why can't she swim?" She read that letter and one week later enrolled in swimming lessons. Now on our annual family water skiing trip each summer she teaches our grandchildren to swim. I have witnessed all this while watching her nurse the highs and lows of recurring rheumatoid arthritis attacks.

I say all this not to glorify my wife but to magnify the Lord, whose indwelling Holy Spirit made all this possible. And lest you think I am exaggerating, let me share the statement of a U.S. federal judge from Louisville, Kentucky. He attended a men's seminar where I spoke, waited until I finished, then identified himself and asked, "Would you give your wife a message for me? I saw her appearance on C-Span when she spoke before the Senate Judiciary Committee on behalf of Judge Robert Bork. I thought her testimony was superb!" And so did I!

## It Works for Anger Too

Meanwhile, back at Forest Home Camp, Beverly called me at home to announce "this wonderful experience I have just had." Then she invited me to come up and hear Dr. Brandt's final message, which I did on Friday at 10:00 A.M. Arriving just as he was being introduced, I settled in a back pew just in time to get blazing mad. Somehow I felt I had been set up. My wife must have told him I was coming, for he no sooner announced his text as Ephesians 4:30-32 than he began to direct his sermon right at me. He told about an angry young minister who had come to him from the Mayo Clinic, where even though he was bleeding inside with ulcers, they "could not find anything organically wrong" and had suggested that he "needed an analyst." He didn't want to see a secular counselor for such a problem, so he called Dr. Brandt, whose clinic at that time was located in Flint, Michigan, 500 miles away. They made three daily appointments.

I identified with this story readily because I was spitting blood. Ulcers ran in my family, so I thought I would treat it myself. Besides, I was too embarrassed to have any of the seven doctors in our church think their pastor was having ulcers.

During his first interview, the young minister exploded. He leaped out of his chair and angrily objected to Dr. Brandt, "I didn't drive 500 miles in a Volkswagen to be insulted!" Then he stormed out and slammed the door. When he returned the next day (after calming down and realizing what a fool he had made of himself), he apologized, and they started in again. The young minister indicated that his church was in the midst of a building campaign—and after all, who could expect a minister to walk in the Spirit during a building campaign? He then outlined all the fights with the Christian education committee over where to locate the Sunday school rooms. Then he had battled the architectural committee over the design of the building, the finance committee over the amount of money to spend, and the trustees on how to spend it. "Last month," he admitted reluctantly, "I even had an altercation with the women's missionary committee!"

I sat in the back, clicking off his responses. We had been in a building campaign for the better part of a year-and-a-half and in one month would dedicate our new church auditorium. I fully recalled the disputes with the Christian education committee over putting Sunday school classrooms in the basement. You see, I grew up in Michigan, where all buildings have basements, but no one includes basements in San Diego buildings, located just a few miles from the San Andreas earthquake fault zone. But if you visit the Scott Memorial Baptist Church, you will find that it is one church in San Diego with a large basement!

In addition, I was educated in the South and had fallen in love with Colonial architecture, but in San Diego, just 17 miles from the Mexican border, Spanish architecture was prevalent. However, if you visit San Diego, you will find one Colonial church there. Does that tell you something?

As Dr. Brandt described his evaluation of this young man as an angry, hostile minister, I heard the message loud and clear. Suddenly I realized that the trustees and architectural committee were not guilty of selfishness and an unyielding spirit. No, their minister was at fault, and for the first time I realized that I had been angry all my life. Yes, I was dedicated to God and had been a very successful pastor for over ten years. I loved God, thoroughly enjoyed His work, and shepherded a wonderful, growing church. *Moody* magazine had even featured a story on the church entitled "The Church That Can't Stop Growing." Twice we had won the award as the fastest-growing Sunday school in California. God had blessed in many areas, but now I was confronted with my angry, sinful nature.

It's difficult to describe my feelings, for I had sincerely tried to be a godly man. From my youth I had worked diligently at purifying my mind so God could use my preaching to help people. But now for the first time I admitted that I was a selfish, anger-filled sinner who insisted on having his own way. As soon as Dr. Brandt concluded his message, I went out among the pine trees to pray and confess my lifelong sin to God. I will never forget that day! For the first time I was consciously filled with the Holy Spirit, who characterized His presence in my life with the most incredible peace I have ever encountered. Suddenly my inner war was over; I had completely surrendered to the Spirit's control.

Guess how long that peace lasted? Two-and-a-half hours! One would think that a minister could have made it three hours at least. But not me. Bev and I hopped into our brand-new car, drove down the mountain, and shared with each other our magnificent experiences with the Spirit of God. Then it happened. Just after hitting the Riverside freeway we passed a sign that read "120 miles to San Diego." One of my pet highway peeves is those idiots who drive in the fourth lane of a freeway, then suddenly decide to get off, cutting right in front of everyone else without looking. And for me it is usually a red sports car.

I was in the third lane cruising at 69½ miles an hour (4½ over the speed limit so we didn't waste time, ½ mile under the "ticket limit"), when that red sports car pulled in front of me. I hit my new power brakes and skidded all over the road. Our car came within an eyelash of flipping over! By the time I got the car under control, *I* was out of control. As my stomach knotted, my mouth loosened, and I loudly declaimed my personal observations about the driver, his parents, and his driver's ed instructor. Almost immediately I recognized that I had grieved the Holy Spirit. I knew instantly because my peace had vanished.

Right there on that freeway I made one of the most important discoveries of my entire spiritual life. Looking up through the windshield of my car, I prayed, "Lord, I've done it again. Please forgive me and fill me with Your Spirit." Instantly the peace returned. Out of the corner of my eye I could see the red lights of his car reaching the stop sign at the end of the off-ramp. That whole process could not have taken more than eight or ten seconds, but in that brief span of time I lost my peace, recognized my sin, confessed it to God, and was restored.

That, I have learned, is the key to the Spirit-filled life. The moment you sin, follow it with your confession and be renewed. Always keep short accounts with God.

I probably had to repeat that formula 100 times the first day. The second day it was much better—about 90 times. Years later I cannot pretend that I never get angry anymore, but it is nothing like it used to be. In fact, a few times I have witnessed an incredible miracle in my life. Cut off by a little red sports car, I have laughed while reflecting on my former reaction. That has to be God at work, for I still possess the same temperament. But now, instead of selfishly indulging my anger, I recognize it as sin that grieves the Holy Spirit. Gradually that lifetime habit has lost its control over my life. The formula for overcoming anger and fear that was recounted in the last chapter will work for anyone, no matter how entrenched and long-lasting.

Many years ago I shared this principle in a Phoenix, Arizona, church. A 70-year-old deacon commented after the service, "Preacher, I should have heard this message 40 years ago. I have been angry all my life. Tell me, is a man of 70 too old to try your formula?" To be honest, I didn't know. So I prayed for wisdom and heard myself quote a relevant Scripture to the gentleman: "With man this is impossible, but with God nothing is impossible to you." And I added, "My God is able to supply all your needs, and the Bible says you can do all things through Christ, who strengthens you." Each time I gave him a Scripture verse, he would stand up a little straighter. Finally he walked away, and I forgot all about the interview—for two years.

One Friday night I was in another Phoenix church and noticed an elderly couple on the right-hand side of the auditorium. After the meeting they introduced themselves, and he reminded me that he was the deacon in that other church two years before. Naturally I was excited to see him and asked how he was doing. He responded, "That's why I came up to talk to you. I wanted to give you a progress report. These have been the best two years of my life. I am a different man! If you don't believe it, here, ask my wife." Turning to the smiling woman, I knew the answer. And that is the acid test to real emotional change—what you are at home.

Interestingly enough, the Bible locates the Spirit-filled (or controlled) life in our home. It is no accident that Ephesians 5:18, the most specific command in the Bible on being filled with the Spirit, forms the introduction to the lengthiest passage in the New Testament on family living. The chapter tells wives how to treat husbands, instructs husbands how to treat their wives, explains that children should obey and honor their parents, and informs fathers of their role as instructors of their children.

God never designed the subject of the Spirit-filled life to be argued over by theologians and denominations. He intended it to be the means of enriching our homes, marriages, and relationships. Evidently it works, for in all the years I have been counseling married people, a Spirit-filled couple has never come in for counseling. Like the rest of us, they will face a myriad of problems in life, but they utilize God's special resources in facing them.

And so can you. After reading this book, I hope and pray that you will use these resources in order to enjoy the kind of family life that God has in store for you.

## A Fear-Filled Woman's Testimony

One of the great blessings I receive from having been a Christian writer these past 33 years is the many appreciative letters sent to me from readers across the country. A woman wrote recently to tell how one of my other books that described this technique for overcoming fear had worked for her. She had been the tragic victim of "what every woman fears." A masked man robbed her home, tied her up, and violated her body. Here is how she describes her recovery:

> The aftermath of this experience has been incredible.... When the reality settled in I found myself totally overwhelmed with fear; I couldn't sleep and when I got to the point where I could stay by myself at home, I darted around the house in an almost maniacal state, looking out each window for the man to return. That is the biggest fear; you are totally convinced that he's waiting around a corner, a tree, behind your car and, in my case, behind any door you get ready to open. Statistics about a criminal never returning to the scene of the crime mean nothing to a victim.... The torment ... was

starting to devour me. I finally went to a therapist, but with no real success. What was becoming clear to me was that the root of my problem was spiritual. I could walk into any bookstore and select a self-help book and address the problem, intellectually, which is what we had been doing in therapy, but this was not touching the fear problem.

Your book is what saved my life—really. My first step was to quit taking the anxiety medication I was prescribed for insomnia. This was difficult, but gave me a feeling of having more control over my life. Then I applied the fear formula in your book. I must have repeated those steps a million times just on the first day. At the end of the week, my husband noticed a remarkable change in my demeanor, in everything! And for the very first time since the attack, I felt at peace; settled down.

I don't know how to thank you except by writing you this letter and by recommending your book to just about everyone I know, which I have! You have opened an entirely new dimension for me, both spiritually and in understanding myself.

The woman above agreed that I could use her story anonymously. Hopefully it will help any person caught in the grip of fear or anger to realize that this formula really works. Try it—with God's help it can change your life.

# Spirit-Controlled
# Emotions

Human beings are incredibly emotional creatures. As complex and diverse as we are, nothing has more influence on our total person than our emotions. In fact, I firmly believe that what we are emotionally is basically what we are. If a person is out of emotional control, he is out of control. And in such a state he will never be able to realize his natural potential.

A successful businessman once boasted to me that he had an IQ of over 150, but he has never reached his potential. He is a miserable husband and a lost cause as a father. He does not lack for intelligence or talent, but his hair-trigger anger ignites at the slightest provocation, sending him out of control much of the time. When he wishes to be charming, butter won't melt in his mouth, but under pressure he will detonate.

He is not alone: Across the world, otherwise loving, kind, and decent people destroy their families through the emotions of anger, fear, pride, envy, etc. This lack of control confirms that the Holy Spirit does not govern the person's life. As Dr. Henry Brandt notes, "Pressure doesn't make your spirit, it reveals your spirit." Our Lord said, "Out of the heart of men [the emotional center] proceed evil thoughts, adulteries, fornications, murders, thefts, covetousness, wickedness, deceit, licentiousness, an evil eye, blasphemy, pride, foolishness" (Mark 7:21,22). In another place we read, "As a person thinks in his heart, so is he [or she]."

We have already reviewed the adverse effect on our physical life generated by the emotions of anger or fear. The previous diagram on page 156 puts it in perspective. That walnut-shaped emotional computer the Bible calls "the heart" is neurologically tied in to all the vital organs of the body.

You have doubtless seen a doctor or chiropractor's display of the spinal system. Wires emanate from the brain, leading from the emotional center at the front of the brain, along the spinal column and out to all the other organs of the body. Those wires are really nerves that register control from the brain to the attached organs. When you are relaxed, enjoying the positive emotions of "love, joy, and peace," your whole body functions properly. But when you entertain negative emotions in your "heart" or emotional center, tension is created in the vital organs.

During our youth we can absorb a good deal of such tension, but as we get older (I prefer the term "mature"), our body will break down at the point of least resistance. This causes the ulcers, high blood pressure, heart attacks, etc., that Dr. McMillen mentions in his book.

There are two sources of emotion in the Christian's heart: "the spirit of man," or our human spirit, and the Spirit of God, the new spiritual nature that enters our life when we are born again by faith in the Lord Jesus Christ. The first is the source of all improper emotions. The other, which Paul identified as "the new man," can only experience beneficial emotions. When cultivated, they will control our natural emotions.

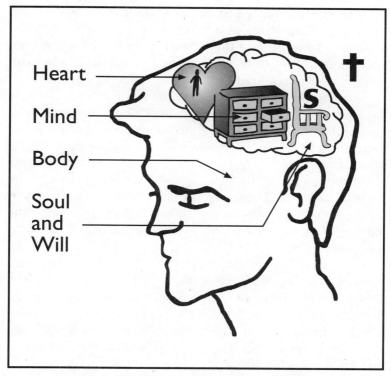

Diagram 9: Four Parts of an Unsaved Person

If a picture is worth a thousand words, the diagram above will more clearly illustrate the concept. Thousands of people have told me after reviewing this presentation that it finally enabled them to understand the two natures for the first time.

This diagram is based on our Lord's statement in Luke 10:27 which separates all four parts of our being, each of which is commanded to love Him—our "heart" (emotional center), "mind," "soul" (our very life, which includes the will), and "strength" (or body).

Close examination of the diagram shows only one nature in the heart—the human nature. An S sits on the throne of the will, which is the seat of our soul. That S stands for SELF. Note also that Christ is symbolized by the cross on the outside of the person. Jesus Christ is not born in our heart. We have to receive Him personally by faith before He will come in.

The above non-Christian can be anyone from a gentle first-grade schoolteacher, a kindly Phlegmatic who loves her children, husband, dog, and neighbors (most of the time) to a Choleric gangster who walks in the flesh all the time. But periodically even the nicest non-Christian will experience selfishly motivated emotions, some of which he cannot control. These egocentric impulses will destroy interpersonal relationships, particularly those with the immediate family. As we have seen, selfishness is always a weapon of destruction.

The diagram on the next page represents the born-again Christian. Notice first that Christ is no longer pictured on the outside of his life. The Savior is now inside, on the throne of the individual's being. When we receive Christ, whether we are fully aware of it or not, we exchange the self-life for the life (lordship) of Christ. We "believe in the Lord Jesus Christ"; and "whoever calls on the name of the Lord shall be saved." Salvation is an exchange of rulers, for repentance causes self-will to abdicate the throne. At the moment of salvation we accept God's will for our life in the form of Christ's Spirit, who comes to rule over us. Therefore He is pictured *on* the throne; self, now the willing servant of Christ, is *under* the throne. (I am indebted to my friend Bill Bright for this helpful throne symbol, which so clearly illustrates rulership.)

The apostle Paul is an excellent biblical illustration of that experience, for on the road to Damascus, intent on carrying out his self-willed desires of persecuting Christians, he fell on his face before Christ and repented. His conversion prayer was very simple: "Lord, what will You have me to do?" In an instant of time he was willing to

Diagram 10: Three Parts of a "Born Again" Christian

exchange his self-will for that of Christ. His new experience is pictured in the above diagram.

Notice the second "man or woman of the heart" symbol. All born-again Christians have this new nature (2 Corinthians 5:17) the moment they are saved. That is their potential for change, including emotional change.

This brings us to the most important point of the entire book: *Receiving Jesus Christ as your Lord and Savior will provide the supernatural power to change.* But what will be modified? Your looks or IQ? No, your emotions! God the Holy Spirit, now working from within, introduces a whole dimension for emotional transformation. Granted, Christians may experience emotional fluctuations according to their natural temperaments, but they will usually enjoy richer, fuller expressions of emotions. They will "rejoice with those who rejoice and weep with those who weep" even more than they did before salvation. The compassion or love of the Holy Spirit can even make the Choleric tenderhearted—and believe me, that takes a miracle! The joy of the Lord can lift the spirit of depression that frequently plagues Melancholies.

Similarly, Sanguines can become more self-controlled, Phlegmatics more motivated. These alterations, however, do not usually happen overnight, nor are they automatic. They occur with maturity and, as we shall see, the cooperation of the individual. This explains why some Christians show a graphic change after salvation, whereas with others it is more gradual, and in some cases they hardly grow at all.

With this in mind, we come to three very popular questions:

1. If I have two natures in me, which one will control my life?

2. How can I tell which nature governs my life at any point in time?

3. How can I walk in the control of the Spirit, as I am commanded in Galatians 5:16-19?

The first answer is simple: *The nature you feed the most will experience the greatest growth!* Notice diagram 10 again. Two natures indwell your heart. God has provided four primary conduits into those two natures—two eyes and two ears. What you put into your mind via these two senses will feed one or the other of the two natures. When you attend church, read a book like this, watch a good Christian program on TV, listen to one on radio, or read your Bible, you are feeding the new nature. If you corrupt your eyes and ears (and thereby your mind and heart) with X-rated movies, dirty TV, or porno books, you will feed your old nature. It is just that simple.

This explains why some Christians seldom grow in their new faith: They fail to impart proper nourishment to the new nature. It also clarifies why a formerly mature Christian can commit a heinous sin that disgraces us all: He or she has gradually fed the old sin nature the wrong material, until the emotions are out of control and the old nature dominates behavior instead of the new. Be sure of this: Whichever nature you feed the most will become the strongest!

For detailed information on nourishing your new nature in a timely way, please consult my book *How to Study the Bible for Yourself.* In it I provide easy-to-use charts that will make Bible study really come to life for you. It also contains a profitable three-year Bible-reading program that will vitalize your spiritual life and supply you with a working knowledge of the Word of God.

The answer to the second question, "How can I tell which nature governs my life?" is even easier: *You will act in accordance with the nature in control.* When you are selfish, angry, or fearful, the old sin nature is running the computer. When you are loving, joyful, and peaceful—especially when the situation or your temperament should propel you in the opposite direction—your new nature is effectively managing control of your emotions.

The diagram on the next page, based on Galatians 5:16-23, illustrates this point. Two primary New Testament passages outline the actions and emotions we can expect from "the flesh," Galatians 5 and Colossians 3. That these are the result of the old nature appears in Galatians 5:19: "The works of the flesh are evident," meaning that the old nature's impact on our lives are clearly revealed by our

**Self in control**

**Christ not given His rightful place**

Diagram 11: The Carnal Christian

deeds. Study the above diagram and the Scriptures cited above.

A quick evaluation of the diagram on the next page suggests that the fleshly nature caused Paul to say, "In me, that is in my flesh, dwells no good thing." This nature, which lives within each of us as long as we remain in the body, creates inestimable damage. We can only handle it through "putting to death" (Colossians 3:5) the deeds of the flesh by starvation. Note also the frightful warning of Galatians 5:21: Those who continue to practice these things "will not inherit the kingdom of God."

This passage clearly teaches that while a Christian may occasionally commit one or more of these actions, he is not going to pursue them continually as a lifestyle. Why? Because he possesses another nature—"the new man," who will make his authority unmistakable by constraining him to do those things that please Christ. If a person does not have *two* spirits in him, he is not a Christian; that is why he will not see the kingdom of God. But once the Spirit enters

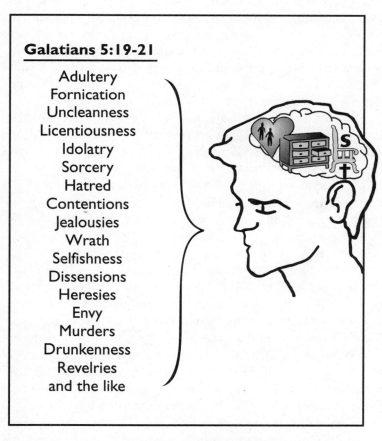

**Galatians 5:19-21**

Adultery
Fornication
Uncleanness
Licentiousness
Idolatry
Sorcery
Hatred
Contentions
Jealousies
Wrath
Selfishness
Dissensions
Heresies
Envy
Murders
Drunkenness
Revelries
and the like

Diagram 12: Weaknesses of the Flesh

his life, He will manifest His presence in a changed lifestyle. This does not mean that he might not occasionally relapse, succumbing to his old ways and forms of behavior. But when he is dedicated to building himself up in his most holy faith, he will become "strong in the Lord." Only then will he enjoy a sturdy spiritual nature which causes him to walk in the Spirit most of the time.

As we have seen, the constant feeding of the old nature while starving the new nature will cause any Christian to lose control and act more like a non-Christian than a believer. One who nurtures the old man continually loses what Paul calls "the war against the Spirit." We can counteract that only by feeding the new nature to the exclusion of the old. This produces a long-range victory over the flesh, but it is not a quick-fix remedy.

What does all this have to do with interpersonal relationships and adjusting to a marriage partner? Everything. The best way to get along with other people, particularly those in your own family, is to gain the emotional control which God the Holy Spirit wants to bestow upon you now that you are a Christian. Diagram 13 reflects the potential for power available to you for overcoming weaknesses by building a strong spiritual life within.

"The fruit of the Spirit is love, joy, peace, longsuffering, kindness, goodness, faithfulness, gentleness, self-control" (Galatians 5:22,23). These nine characteristics of the Spirit in your life guarantee two things: emotional control and strength for overcoming your weaknesses. The first three fruits—love, joy, and peace—are obviously the emotions that provide a spiritual antidote to lack of emotional control through such hostile emotions as anger, wrath, or malice, and the fear emotions of anxiety, worry, or dread. Even depression is offset by joy. Spirit-controlled Christians are never out of control emotionally. They may undergo emotional upheavals amid the traumas and sorrows of life, but they are not overcome. According to Paul, "We are

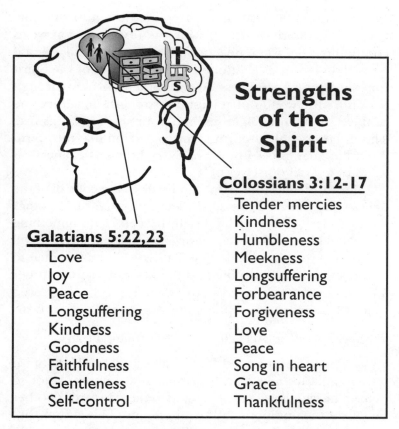

**Strengths of the Spirit**

**Colossians 3:12-17**
Tender mercies
Kindness
Humbleness
Meekness
Longsuffering
Forbearance
Forgiveness
Love
Peace
Song in heart
Grace
Thankfulness

**Galatians 5:22,23**
Love
Joy
Peace
Longsuffering
Kindness
Goodness
Faithfulness
Gentleness
Self-control

Diagram 13: Strengths of the Spirit

distressed on every hand but not forsaken." There is victory for the child of God through the indwelling ministry of the Holy Spirit.

The nine fruits of the Spirit also provide a strength for every human weakness. That was graphically illustrated as I taught a Biblical Psychology course at Christian Heritage College several years ago. I asked the 65 seniors and juniors, all counseling majors, to help me name all the weaknesses people have that will someday confront them in the counseling room.

After we listed 84 weaknesses, I pointed them to the nine fruits of the Spirit, which provide the resources that we as counselors need when dealing with Christians, and asked if we could identify at least one fruit or strength of the Spirit for every human weakness. As we worked our way through the entire list, we found at least two strengths for every one of the 84 human weaknesses, and at times as many as five. This discovery only confirmed my conviction that the Spirit-filled life guarantees power for every human weakness—if we want to avail ourselves of it.

The third question, "How can I walk in the control of the Spirit?" has been addressed in detail in some of my other books, so I will only sketch it briefly here. It is not something that should be glossed over, however, for it is not only the will of God for your life (Ephesians 5:17,18) but an essential to the successful Christian life and the key to learning proper adjustment to one's marriage partner. The following seven steps will help you appropriate this experience as your own.

*1. Self-examination* (Acts 20:28; 1 Corinthians 11:28).

A Christian interested in the filling of the Holy Spirit must regularly "take heed" to "examine himself"—not to determine whether he measures up to the standards of other people or the traditions and requirements of his church, but whether he manifests the previously mentioned results of being filled with the Holy Spirit. If he lacks the power to witness, fails to reflect a joyful, submissive spirit, or finds the nine temperament traits of the Holy Spirit deficient in his life, self-examination will uncover his besetting sins. Identified sin can be handled in only one way:

*2. Confess all known sin* (1 John 1:9).

> If we confess our sins, He is faithful and just to forgive us our sins and to cleanse us from all unrighteousness.

After examining ourselves in the light of the Word of God, we should confess all sin brought to mind by the Holy Spirit, including those characteristics of the Spirit-filled life that we lack. Until we acknowledge as sin the absence of compassion, lack of self-control, need for humility, anger instead of gentleness, bitterness instead of kindness, and unbelief instead of faith, we will never experience the filling of the Holy Spirit. However, the moment we recognize these deficiencies as sin and confess them to God, He will "cleanse us from all unrighteousness." Once we have been made clean vessels through the Spirit's cleansing, we are prepared for the filling of the Holy Spirit. God only occupies clean vessels (2 Timothy 2:21).

*3. Yield yourself completely to God* (Romans 6:12,13).

> Do not let sin reign in your mortal body, that you should obey it in its lusts. And do not present your members as instruments of unrighteousness to sin, but present yourselves to God as being alive from the dead, and your members as instruments of righteousness to God.

This step is probably bypassed by more Christians than any other. They submit to God, but not on a 100 percent basis. For some reason, many Christians seem reluctant to yield everything to their Lord, preferring to withhold a small portion of life to themselves. They fail to realize that this will keep them from ever being filled with the Holy Spirit. Remember, God will not share your affection with another. As the hymnwriter described it, "What shall I give Thee, Master? . . . Not just a part, nor half of my heart—I will give all to Thee." God is not satisfied with 97 percent of your life; He demands a 100 percent compliance. Perhaps we forget that God is no man's debtor; we cannot outgive Him. The more of yourself you give, the more He blesses.

The best bargain you will ever make is to yield your total self to Him.

Do not make the mistake of holding back on God! Romans 8:32 tells us, "He who did not spare His own Son, but delivered Him up for us all, how shall He not with Him also freely give us all things?" If God loved us so much that He sent His Son to die for us, surely He is interested in nothing but our good; therefore we can trust Him with our lives. You will never find a miserable Christian in the center of God's will!

Ephesians 5:18 admonishes, "Do not be drunk with wine . . . but be filled with the Spirit." When a person is drunk, he is dominated by alcohol. So it is with the filling of the Spirit: We are controlled by God. For consecrated Christians this is often a major determination, for we can always find some worthy purpose for our lives, not realizing that we are becoming filled with ourselves rather than the Holy Spirit.

When you give your life to God, do not attach any strings or conditions to it. He is such a God of love that you can safely give yourself to Him without reservation, knowing that His plan is far better than yours. And remember, the attitude of submission is absolutely necessary for the filling of God's Spirit. Your will is the will of the flesh, and the Bible warns that "the flesh profits nothing."

Someone has suggested that being yielded to the Spirit is being available to the Spirit. Peter and John in Acts 3 provide an example of that availability. They were on their way to the temple to pray when they saw the lame man begging alms. Because they were sensitive to the Holy Spirit, they healed him "in the name of Jesus Christ of Nazareth." The man began leaping about and praising God until a crowd gathered. Still sensitive to the Holy Spirit, Peter began to preach, and "many of those who heard the word believed; and the number of the men came to be about five thousand" (Acts

4:4). We are not told whether Peter and John ever entered the temple to pray, for God had other plans.

Many times we are so engrossed in some beneficial Christian activity that we are not available to the prompting of the Spirit. When a Christian yields himself to God "as those that are alive from the dead," he takes time to obey the Spirit's direction and submits his emotions to the Holy Spirit's control.

*4. Ask to be filled with the Holy Spirit* (Luke 11:13).

> If you then, being evil, know how to give good gifts to your children, how much more will your heavenly Father give the Holy Spirit to those who ask Him!

When a Christian has examined himself, confessed all known sin, and yielded himself without reservation to God, he is then ready to fulfill one final requirement—asking to be filled with the Holy Spirit. We are not taught to fast and pray or beg God to be filled with the Spirit. We must simply meet His conditions and then ask to be controlled by His Spirit.

The Lord Jesus compares this to our treatment of earthly children. Certainly a good father would not make his children beg for something he commanded them to do. How much less does God make us implore Him to be filled with the Holy Spirit. But don't forget Step 5.

*5. Believe that you are filled with the Holy Spirit! And thank Him for His filling.*

> But he who doubts is condemned if he eats, because he does not eat from faith; for whatever is not from faith is sin (Romans 14:23).

> In everything give thanks, for this is the will of God in Christ Jesus for you (1 Thessalonians 5:18).

For many Christians the battle is won or lost right here. After examining, confessing, yielding, and asking for His filling, they are faced with a vital decision: believing that they are filled or departing in unbelief, in which case they have sinned, for "whatever is not of faith is sin."

The same Christian who tells the new convert to "take God at His Word concerning salvation" often finds it difficult to heed his own advice concerning the filling of the Holy Spirit. If you have fulfilled the first four steps, then by faith thank God for His filling. Don't wait for feelings or physical signs; fasten your faith to the Word of God, which is independent of feelings. Believing we are filled with the Spirit is merely taking God at His Word, and that is the only absolute in this world (Matthew 24:35). Then watch for His control over your emotions. If you are a hostile person by nature, love, joy, and peace will spontaneously spring up in the face of events that formerly caused you to experience anger. And when faith replaces fear, that is the work of the Holy Spirit.

*6. Read the Word of God daily.*

It is not possible to "walk in the Spirit" (Galatians 5:16) on a continuing basis, as we are commanded, unless we read the Word of God regularly. Spiritual strength to overcome the temptations and desires of the flesh is imparted through the Word. Just as ingesting food gives the body strength to work, play, and live, so "eating" the Word through Bible reading and study will strengthen you to enjoy the Spirit-controlled life every day.

*7. Avoid grieving or quenching the Holy Spirit through anger and fear.*

Nothing short-circuits the ministry of the Holy Spirit in the life of the believer faster than grieving Him through anger or quenching Him through fear. When you do revert to old habits, immediately confess them as sin and again ask for His filling. Above all, keep short accounts, repeating these seven steps every time you need them, at first several times a day. Gradually you will begin in the morning with them and go the entire day, reusing them only once or twice. Eventually you will become a different person emotionally and spiritually. In time your greatest joy will be the continual evidence of God's Spirit in your life, giving you emotional control and strength in overcoming your biggest weaknesses.

# *Avoid Criticism Like the Plague*

The more you love a person, the more you desire his praise. Conversely, criticism of the person with whom you share your life is devastating. For that reason, all couples should learn the art of praise rather than blame.

No one gives lessons in criticism; that seems to be an art form that arises naturally. However, some temperaments are more "gifted" in this than others. But the universal need of all temperaments is approval, never condemnation. Nothing destroys love faster than a continuous barrage of criticism. As I travel the country, men repeatedly complain, "She is just too critical, even about unimportant matters."

Recently I spoke at a couple's banquet in a church here in Washington and was intrigued by the excellent testimony given by a couple who detailed how their conversion had kept them from the divorce court. The man, spokesman for the two, was recounting their experience when his wife whispered something to him. He stopped and corrected himself by saying, "I'm sorry, it was when our youngest child was 3½ years old" (he had originally said five years old). I would ask,

"Who cares?" If she is that corrective on everything, even conversion won't guarantee a happy marriage relationship.

As we have noted, Sanguines, who have little concern for detail, often marry Melancholies, who are apt to be nit-pickers if they indulge themselves. And that is the big IF. They need not indulge each urge to correct their partner; they can learn to keep criticism to themselves. You have undoubtedly heard a Sanguine give directions only to be corrected by the spouse, "No, it's two miles" or "Go to the second traffic light." Again, what does it matter?

A wife returned from a party where her Sanguine husband had kept the guests in stitches all evening with an endless series of humorous stories. As soon as the door closed, she attacked. He was "casual and cavalier" with details—and then she proceeded to list all his inaccuracies. He simply responded, "They enjoyed them, didn't they?" Like the Sanguine-Melancholy couple mentioned earlier in the book, the difference in these two is very basic: She tells stories for accuracy and information, he for effect. He excuses "little exaggerations" as means to a comic end. She considers it "lying."

A perfectionist mate tends to stiffen when her "obviously inaccurate" partner is called on to pray in church. She may consider him spiritually unqualified because of his "lying tendency." He in turn protests that she is overly critical. In a sense they are both right. Once two partners have talked openly about this, one should not try to play Holy Spirit by correcting a mate all the time. Men particularly have a difficult time with wifely criticism. They desperately need respect from their wives, as Paul makes clear in Ephesians 5:33 when he reminds Christian wives to "see that you respect your husband." A perfectionist has a difficult time granting respect to anyone who reflects obvious imperfections. He fails to realize that no one can measure up to his standard of perfection, not even himself.

In a situation like this, communication between the partners comes to a screeching halt. Early in our marriage I became aware that Bev is a planner, whereas I am an idea person. I can propagate an idea a minute; she analyzes it. One day she tactfully inquired, "Why am I the last person in the church to learn what you are planning to do?" It really hadn't occurred to me that such was the case, but when she offered several illustrations, I could see her point.

"Do you really want to know?" I asked. "Of course." So I gently pointed out that every time I came up with an idea, she would shoot holes in it—primarily because she can anticipate some of the pitfalls I will encounter in pursuit of my plans. Since I focus initially on the whole rather than the parts, I like to talk out my ideas with associates and get their feedback. Because I was their pastor, such people would very discreetly make suggestions that shaped a project, and by the time I had talked it over with six or eight people, I was able to formulate a program and take it to the appropriate board. Because my youthful ego couldn't stand Bev's criticism, subconsciously I avoided any discussions with her, and she would be the last to learn.

From that day on she changed her tactic. She went out of her way to compliment me on "my clever idea"; then, after evaluating it, she would offer positive suggestions. Gradually I found her a positive receptacle for my plans and began to welcome her incisive input. Today she is without question not only my best friend but my best sounding board for new ideas. You can't imagine what that has done to our communication level. We can hardly find time to discuss all the activities going on in each other's professional world, in addition to the events in our family world.

## Try Praise!

A very popular book on administration is entitled *The One-Minute Manager*. Essentially the book challenges a manager to praise all his people one minute a day. After that, if he has to correct them, at least they heard more than criticism from him that day.

That principle is biblical. If you doubt it, do a Bible study on the subject of praise. After thanking and praising God for all He has done, we can render approval to people for their praiseworthy deeds. As you read the epistles of Paul, notice his use of that technique. The book of Philemon is a case in point. He begins with praise ("I thank my God"), then gradually builds to his request: Philemon, receive the returning runaway slave as a son now that he is converted.

Criticism does nothing for a relationship. Give yourself to praise if you wish your love to blossom. This is particularly necessary for a man. If he fails to commend his wife, she will develop an impaired self-image. Men usually gain their self-acceptance from their vocation, a wife from her husband. If he praises her and makes his friends realize how much he values her as a person, she will accept herself as a woman. If he disapproves of her, he will destroy her self-acceptance.

Eleven tragedies in my counseling ministry stand out in my mind. All had the same problem: A wife and mother left her husband and children to run off with another man. These situations featured one common denominator: The husband criticized the wife, not only to her face but in front of his friends. That is the most devastating attack a man can make on a woman. Many a defeated and often desperate woman has responded when her husband bragged at never striking her, "A thousand times I had rather he had hit me instead of constantly criticizing or disapproving everything I did!"

I am so convinced of a man's ability to enrich a woman's life by his "verbal stroking" through praise and compliments that I have developed the following theory: "A woman's self-acceptance five years into their marriage is a reflection of her husband's loving treatment." The only exception is a woman who comes to marriage out of a terrible background of physical (including sexual) abuse, constant criticism, or inordinate legalism. In such cases it may take ten years of loving husband treatment to help her realize her true worth. But sooner or later, what her husband thinks of her, good or bad, will be the principal cause of her self-acceptance or self-rejection.

Women need love! That is why God commanded husbands to "love your wife" four times in the New Testament. The God who made women and knows their greatest need raised up husbands to provide it for them.

# Accept
# Your Partner's
# Temperament

By this time you should be convinced that the many differences between you and your partner are not unique. Some are caused by background, others by the differences between the sexes. But the most significant ones may stem from contrasting temperaments. In all probability, that would be the case no matter whom you married.

One significant blessing that married couples gain from temperament study is an explanation as to why a partner makes the decisions, reflects prejudices, or expresses the preferences he does. Understanding temperament will help you with the "why," but only the Lord can assist you with the adjustment process.

One woman married to an accountant (most of whom have a good dose of Melancholy temperament) was irritated by her husband's constant "checkup policy." The family budget granted her an allowance for food, sundries, and clothing each month. She opened her own checking account to handle the transaction, so a bank balance each month measured her success. She was irritated most by her husband's insistence that he check her work each month to make sure she balanced. She considered this an invasion of privacy and felt he had no right to make such a demand. When she read

*Spirit-Controlled Temperament,* she began to realize that her Melancholy husband was "a checker-upper" on everyone, which made his persistence somewhat easier to accept.

Then one April, while he was doing tax returns for some friends, she stood in the doorway of the dining room and watched him add a column of figures on the form. Even though he used a calculator, he wrote the answer on a sheet of paper, turned it over, added it again, entered that tabulation on a scrap of paper, turned it over, and repeated the process a third time. Then he compared all three answers. Finding them in agreement, he smiled and entered the triple-checked answer in the appropriate box on the form. Suddenly it dawned on her: "He doesn't just check up on me and everyone else—he even checks up on himself!" That realization didn't change anything, but it did help her to accept a temperament trait.

By studying the temperaments, you can determine your partner's temperament and work with it, not against it. It would also be helpful for you and your partner to take the temperament test we have developed (ordering information may be found at the end of this book). It will clarify many interesting characteristics about each other and offer additional suggestions on how to realize your potential. Most of all, it accurately identifies both your primary and secondary temperaments. Once you know your temperament and that of your partner, you will more easily accept each other and work together rather than clash over differences. Most weaknesses come from a person's primary temperament, with about 20 to 30 percent arising from the secondary temperament. The following suggestions will help you to accept your partner's weaknesses, particularly those that you find most difficult to bear.

*1. Admit that you have weaknesses too.*

Humility is the best possible base for establishing any relationship between two people. That is true particularly in marriage because the couple spends so much time together. True love for another person rests on a humble spirit.

A healthy look at your own temperament will enable you to recognize that you have brought more than strengths into your marriage and that God is not finished with you yet. He is strengthening your weaknesses and improving you all the time. In fact, you probably have a long way to go. Realistically facing that fact will help you to accept Step 2.

The Bible quite clearly insists that our greatest problems emanate from pride—the exact opposite of humility. Passages in James and 1 Peter warn us that the devil is a roaring lion that goes about seeking whom he may devour. Most Christians identify that statement with lust, greed, or other carnal passions. But in both contexts the issue is *lack of humility*—or pride—that makes us vulnerable to the fiery darts of the devil. Several years ago I published a book, which is now out of print, entitled *If Ministers Fall, Can They Be Restored?* During the exhaustive research on the subject, I was intrigued to learn that the most common cause of their fall was not pornography or evil fantasies but *pride,* which exposes a person to all kinds of serious sins, chief among them being intolerance of another person's weaknesses.

The individual who is humble enough to recognize that he is not perfect is best able to: 1) become motivated toward self-improvement and 2) accept the imperfections of others.

*2. Accept the fact that your partner—and everyone else's—is not perfect.*

One of the complications to the adjustment phase of marriage (the first three to seven years) is that subconsciously most people naively overlook the partner's weaknesses. Even worse, as one lady stated, "I knew Tom wasn't perfect, but I thought I could whip him into shape after we were married." She had not anticipated that his mother had tried before her and failed, and thus her endeavors met with an incredible amount of resistance. The most cruel blow was his oft-repeated statement, "I didn't need a mother when I married you—I already had one!" A surprising number of people, consciously or subconsciously, plan to renovate their partner after the honeymoon. Rarely does that work! Learn to accept your partner unconditionally, and never fantasize about that "absolute angel" you could have married. Such an individual might also have feet of clay. Everyone is a repository of weaknesses, so you would do well to accept those of your partner.

### 3. Confront your partner once, in love, with his/her weaknesses.

If your partner's weaknesses grate on you, and after trying to ignore them, heed the advice of Ephesians 4:15 and "speak the truth in love." Usually you can gently confront your partner with the area of irritation only one time—so do it carefully. For example, "Ralph, honey, would you mind if I shared something you do that bothers me?" Most people, out of curiosity if for no other reason, will agree, so move ahead, and with moderation but without heat express your concern. Don't be surprised if you arouse an angry response that includes self-defense or denial. But do not argue; just leave it there. What you want is not a verbal agreement but a change in behavior. Let him think about it. Then . . .

### 4. Commit the problem to God.

Christians are very fortunate. We have a court of last appeals which can be petitioned when we run into trouble. If God challenges us to "make our wants and wishes" known, why not a change in the behavior of our partner? Prayer solicits God's power to effect that modification, and it helps to settle in our mind that we have taken appropriate steps toward change. Now we can leave the matter with Him. Don't bring it up again lest you find yourself guilty of nagging—and that never works.

*5. Work with, not against, your partner's weaknesses—and never criticize what you see as temperament weaknesses.*

Whatever your partner's temperament, bear in mind that you made the choice. A man gave me a card which read, "Never criticize your wife; it's a reflection on your judgment." As long as you remain critical of your partner's temperament-induced behavior patterns, you will experience conflict. A woman reported recently, "My husband and I irritate each other." Why? Because neither would let the other be himself.

The closest temperaments I have ever counseled were a self-acknowledged Chlor-San husband and a Chlor-Mel wife. (Personally, I thought she was a Mel-Chlor, but I don't argue with people about their self-evaluations.) In any case, she admired this dynamic, industrious, forceful man, "except for one thing. He is sarcastically cruel to anyone who gets in his way, particularly the children." (Choleric husbands are often accused of overshooting the field when disciplining children.) He complained, "She is cold and unloving unless I'm perfect. I'm tired of getting loved as a reward for good behavior." (Leave it to a Choleric to tell it like it is!)

Two angry people living in the same house will inevitably produce conflict. That kind of problem must be approached in two ways: He must face his anger as sin, and she, with God's help, must accept him, whether he achieves victory or not. They could also treat each other kindly, of course, to avoid precipitating conflict. Usually one has little trouble picking a fight if he wants to, but Jesus said, "Blessed are the peacemakers."

It is absolutely imperative that both spouses learn how to approach each other in light of their respective temperaments. Hopefully, not all couples are as different as my wife and I. No matter what needs to be done, we can always expect to prefer different ways of doing it. If we're planning a trip, Bev thinks we should take the northern route, whereas I opt for the southern. She drives too slow by my standards, but I go too fast by hers. Incidentally, we solved that by establishing a firm rule: "He that holds the steering wheel makes the decision—the other keeps quiet." We don't even shop alike. Bev buys just what we need; I hate to waste my time going to the store without filling up the cart. It used to irritate her that I always brought home far more than the grocery list; now she recognizes my weakness as the price of not doing the shopping herself.

We don't even make decisions in the same length of time. I can usually make up my mind in eight-tenths of a second; Bev likes to mull things over, analyze them from all sides, and then come to a conclusion. In this regard, I have learned that my snap judgments that may work out in the long run are not always the best route to take. With that realization has come an increasing respect for her judgment because she thinks things through. When I am confronted with a decision, she has learned to suggest, "Let's think about it." At first that used to bug me; now I'm discovering that her delaying tactic often saves time. On the other hand, I have learned never to force her into a quick decision, for it will almost always be negative. If I plan further in advance and say, "Honey, there's something I'd like you to think about—don't give me an answer now," she usually will come around to my way of thinking or offer a profitable suggestion to improve "our" idea.

Study your partner. Find his likes, dislikes, prejudices, and weaknesses. Then try to avoid pushing or demanding in those areas. Isn't that love? Like paint, love covers a multitude of sins. Selfishness always demands its own way—but ruins a relationship in getting it. Besides, partners always do better together!

When Bev and I approach a trip, she plans in detail for weeks in advance. I try to get as much work done right up until the last minute, then chart the trip as it unfolds. For example, we were scheduled to drive to Detroit on vacation with our four children. Before leaving, I had to preach three morning and two evening services, so I was kept mentally busy until church was over. I had arranged for two top carriers for our station wagon to house all the luggage; this was one trip that would provide enough room for everyone to move around in the car without feeling cramped. So I hurried home, packed the suitcases inside the top carriers, and proudly announced at 11 P.M. that we were ready to go. I am a night person, so I wanted to get 400 miles out of the way while the family slept. Then in the morning Bev could take over while I rested. That had been a successful pattern for several years.

As I backed out of the driveway to begin this 2450-mile trip, I turned to Bev and asked, "Honey, would you look in the glove compartment and see if I have a map in there?" She had every right to exclaim, "You stupid idiot! Do you mean to say you haven't even studied a map to know which way we're going?" (There were several choices.) But that is not her style. Besides, she knows by now that a spouse who attempts to live two lifetimes at the same time seldom has minutes left over for trivial details. Instead, she reached down into her traveling bag and pulled out the AAA trip map she had sent for. Their experts had made all the choices for us, advising the best routes to take, and I had to confess that her advance planning had "made the trip." She admitted in kind that my scheming to get all the luggage up on top turned out to be an enjoyable contribution as well. Now you can understand why I say, as married couples, "we do better together!"

# *Two Doors to Slam*

Before we take one more step toward marital adjustment, two doors must be nailed shut. Hopefully they are not open for you.

First is the door of divorce. Whenever two people in need of adjusting consider the possibility of divorce as a viable option, it becomes a hindrance to the adjustment process. If you are a Christian, divorce is not an alternative choice—unless, of course, your partner has been unfaithful. That is the one exception which our Lord has given (Matthew 19:9).

Long before the threat of AIDS and other sexually transmitted diseases, I advised Christians to file for divorce on the grounds of adultery if they had conclusive proof of their partner's unfaithfulness. They were not obligated to complete the process of divorce if the partner truly repented and was willing to recommit himself to the sexual fidelity pledged on their wedding day. But it is very important that sexual deviants are confronted immediately with their sin; otherwise they develop the world's sinful attitude toward adultery: "It's no big deal!"

I am here to tell you that it *is* a big deal! It is probably the most searing, debilitating, destructive calamity that one partner can bestow upon another. Marriage is a sexual contract, a covenant between two people and almighty God made in front of invited witnesses—a contract to a lifetime of sexual exclusivity. The minute that pledge is broken, they have severed their commitment. In the Old Testament such individuals were to be taken out and stoned to death, which reflects the seriousness of the crime in the eyes of God.

Permitting a spouse to show disrespect and lack of commitment by having sex with someone else is not only morally, spiritually, and emotionally destructive but extremely dangerous physically. I have dealt with more than a few cases in which a single unfaithful experience introduced herpes or AIDS into the relationship, impairing the couple's life.

Admittedly, the Bible is strong on forgiveness, and so am I. But filing for divorce on the grounds of adultery will get a person's attention. After extensive counseling with your pastor or other spiritual leaders, you determine your only alternative is that your partner sincerely repent or other appropriate action may be taken. Unfortunately, too many Christians, both men and women, are inclined to let a partner get away with this sin with a slap on the wrist— which usually makes it easier for him to repeat it.

Short of infidelity, I see no other grounds for divorce in the Bible. This does not mean that a woman must stay with a man who loses control through anger, alcohol, or drugs and beats her. In such cases I advise a woman to go to court and get a restraining order to protect her life. Abusive men need to realize that legal representatives will impose restraint. Naturally, I advise such couples, after due repentance and promise that a recurrence will not take place, to reestablish their marriage based on forgiveness and love. But the man who beats his wife without accountability will be more inclined to repeat the offense when provoked. Dr. James Dobson has covered these issues in greater detail in his excellent book *Love Must Be Tough*. I heartily recommend it.

Regardless of the differences between two people, God intends them to remain together. But with a divorce rate above 50 percent today, it is more fashionable for those facing adjustment or "personality conflicts" to choose what they consider the easy way out. Eventually that "easy way" proves to be much more cumbersome and arduous than anticipated.

Just entertaining the idea that divorce is "a way of escape" makes it more difficult for couples to find a solution for their differences within the marriage relationship. First Corinthians 7:27 asks, "Are you bound to a wife? Do not seek to be loosed." This does not mean that a couple must be committed to a lifetime of *conflict* because of their differences; it does suggest that they seek *conflict resolution* by applying some of the techniques given in this book, leading them toward marital adjustment.

## Dump the Third Party

The second inhibitor to a good adjustment, if it exists, is the third person. Get rid of that individual. Married love is different from paternal love, which allows one to extend love to several children at the same time. Because of the highly sexual aspect of marriage, the human heart cannot love two people of the opposite sex equally. Nothing complicates normal marital adjustment like the presence of a third person.

When one partner leaves a mate—particularly when the wife leaves her children—I will ask, "Are you interested in someone else?" Almost invariably the answer is yes. Often the presence of that third person has given the troubled partner the courage to leave home and conclude that it is time to terminate the marriage. Frankly, I have had absolutely no success in reconciling a couple while one of them has contact with a third party.

The first matter of business in any restoration process is to dump the outsider. Unfortunately, one of the married partners may be genuinely in love with that person, and may have developed a sexual intimacy even before the separation occurred. But in every case the existence of a third party is not of God! The Bible is clear that married partners should "cleave unto each other"—not to a third person. As traumatic as it may be, the third party must be sent packing and the two should never see each other again. I have extensive case file evidence that this act of faith, expelling the illegitimate lover, can be followed by a time of adjustment and then a new, growing love based on commitment and the will of God. All of us need God's help to keep our love alive, but we cannot expect divine assistance outside the bounds of faithfulness.

A woman in the Northwest became romantically enthralled with a "Don Juan" lothario who featured an out-of-control libido. Her husband was a staid, dependable, unexciting school administrator. His idea of a weekend away from professional duties was to sleep in on Saturday morning, mope around the house till lunch, putter in the garage during the afternoon, attend church Sunday morning, and enjoy a nap Sunday afternoon. Obviously he was a ball of fire! Sexually he could "take it or leave it"—a most dangerous policy for a man to follow. By the time I was brought into the situation, she had already slept with "Don Juan" several times.

Fortunately her husband was willing to forgive and attempt to activate his Phlegmatic self. After much persuasion, the wife admitted that the relationship with "Don" was sinful and that God would never bless her life until she returned to her husband and two children. However, her passion for "Don" was so intense that I had her call me on the phone whenever she felt inclined to see him again. Her desire to live a godly life finally overcame her passion, and today she has a healthy marriage, for which she thanks me whenever I am speaking in her area.

God's way is always best, but it is an act of faith. I write this as I sadly return from a situation in which the wife contracted herpes from the three-time marital loser she is convinced she loves. Somehow she is persuaded that leaving her husband and two boys will prove to this professional bed-hopper that he will be happy in her bed for the rest of his life. One day, we can readily prophesy, she will be abandoned, alone, depressed, and probably even more diseased. Unwilling to trust her future to God and return to a husband who has the capacity to be a good and faithful partner, she defies the laws of God at her own peril. For her the future is now. Little does she realize that her worst days are yet to come.

## Hopefully

Hopefully, none of the above chapter applies to you. Instead, you are interested in learning to adjust to your opposite partner—and that is what we will consider throughout the rest of this book.

# *Apologize and Forgive*

I wish I could say that I have never displeased my wife or done anything for which I had to apologize, but that would be a lie. I have given my wife more than enough cause to be offended for the rest of our lives, and she has rankled me more than a few times. But all such transgressions have been confessed and forgiven long ago.

The Bible enjoins us, "Confess your trespasses to one another" (James 5:16). While that concerns all interpersonal relationships, it is nowhere more appropriate than in the marriage union. According to an old saying, "You always hurt the one you love." "Always" may be too strong, but we do cause injury all too often, mainly because we share so much time together. And because we love each other, we have the capacity to hurt more severely.

For these and other reasons, we must prepare on a daily basis to repeat the two most difficult-to-pronounce words in the language: "I'm sorry." An apology does two things: It removes any potential root of bitterness in the offended heart before it can grow into a giant tree, and it tends to diffuse wrath.

The Bible teaches, "A soft answer turns away wrath." Have you ever incurred your partner's resentment, been reprimanded, and then, instead of arguing, turned to him or her and said, "You're right! I shouldn't have done that. Will you forgive me?" That will always take the air out of someone's sails. I don't suggest you do it as a tactic, but sincerely confess your fault when you have done wrong, even when your partner's reaction is equally as wrong as your deed. Often the irate partner will not only forgive you but will ask forgiveness for words uttered in retaliation. Apologies always clear the air.

## Apologize, Don't Compensate

My dear parents rarely apologized to each other, as I recall. They had been raised in that old school which stipulated that the offended partner should be mollified by receiving something that would please him.

I well remember my father's apologies—and hated them! Whenever he offended my mother, he would say, "Margaret, next Sunday after church, let's go for a ride. I'll take you to the cemetery." He knew that Mom enjoyed a visit to her mother's grave, a few tears, and then a return to the car with "I feel so much better!" I liked my mother's apologies much better. She would make up to my father by baking him a three-layer German chocolate cake, and we all shared the moment. They could have saved all that gasoline and all those calories if they had learned to look at each other and utter sincerely, "Honey, I'm sorry I offended you. Please forgive me." It would take a heart of stone to reject such an offer.

Unfortunately, many couples are too proud, hurt, or offended to confess when they have caused pain. Yet the Lord Himself tied confession of sins to successful worship when He taught, "If you bring your gift to the altar [act of worship], and there remember that your brother has something against you, leave your gift there before the altar, and go your way. First be reconciled to your brother [or partner], and then come and offer your gift" (Matthew 5:23-25).

Correcting offenses between partners or friends was so important to God that He declared it an essential preface to worship. Yet I fear that many Christian couples head for church so angry that they can't speak. No wonder children grow up identifying Christians as hypocrites. They desperately need to see their parents demonstrate forgiveness. They can understand that their parents are human enough to offend each other occasionally and they don't expect parents to be perfect, but they should be raised within a spirit of reconciliation.

Leon Jaworsky, the Houston Texas attorney who was appointed as prosecutor of the Watergate scandal, wrote an article on forgiveness that appeared in *Moody* magazine. He attended church one Sunday morning here in Washington during the height of the investigations. He had spent hours listening to the now-infamous "Watergate tapes" and had concluded from those crass and profane conversations that President Nixon was a far more evil-hearted man than he had ever imagined. Suddenly into the silent attitude of worship just prior to the beginning of the service, the doors burst open and the Secret Service flooded the room. President Nixon and his wife were ushered to the front row.

Jaworsky admitted that he instinctively responded, "That hypocrite! How could he be so vile at the White House and then march in here piously, pretending to worship?" But almost immediately his thoughts were engulfed by shame and remorse as he looked up beyond the pulpit at the beautiful stained-glass window that revealed the Savior in the Garden of Gethsemane, sweating drops of blood for our sins. Suddenly he found himself confessing to God. After all, he mused, perhaps this troubled soul has come here to gain forgiveness too. As soon as the Watergate prosecutor sought God's forgiveness, he was prepared to extend it to another human being who needed the forgiving touch of God—even a fallen president.

Everyone needs forgiveness, not once but many times. All happy marriages share one common characteristic—forgiveness. But remember, it is always easier to forgive if the offender apologizes. We are commanded to forgive whether he does or not. You cannot decide whether your partner will forgive, but you can make the decision for yourself.

Actually, I have good and bad news about apologies. The good news is that when we sin against or offend our partners, we can be forgiven—if we apologize. The bad news is that if we don't make amends, the affront will grow well out of proportion to the act. As an antidote to resentment, frustration, and burgeoning antagonism, develop the therapy of apology and forgiveness.

# Put On the Seven Christian Virtues

Everyone expects Christians to be different. Even the media hold Christians to a higher moral standard of behavior than they do unbelievers. Over a decade ago we saw a classic example of this right in our nation's capital. Two veteran Congressmen were caught in sex scandals with congressional pages (who were minors). One, a professing Christian with a strong conservative voting record, was apprehended with a 17-year-old girl young enough to be his daughter. The other, a liberal and an avowed homosexual, was arrested while sodomizing a 17-year-old boy. Both were rebuked by the ethics committee, and both apologized to Congress and the voters. The homosexual was reelected by his Massachusetts constituency three times and still serves in Congress. The professing Christian was defeated by his Illinois voters. Why? Because the Christian failed to live up to the standard of behavior expected of him.

Today, far more serious allegations go all the way to the White House, not only of sexual promiscuity but also using the most powerful office in the world as a power base to impose sexual favors on devoted followers. Many Americans, particularly women voters, seem unconcerned and actually believe that what the president does in his private life shouldn't concern us. This shows how much liberal humanism in our entertainment industry and in our educational system for 40 years have eroded our nation's values. It could be said that liberals do not hold their leaders to *any* moral standard.

That same attitude is reflected in the sex scandals of TV ministers and the fall of local pastors. Yet of all the major professions in the world, the ministry has the lowest percentage of those who commit adultery—or who are presented with greater temptation. However, ministers are automatically held to a higher moral standard of behavior than any other professional, and rightly so, for they are Christians. God Himself commanded us to "be holy even as I am holy!"

## How to Turn Christian Young People Off

The best way I know to alienate Christian young people from Christ and His church is to fail to live in the home what you profess and hear at church. Young people, particularly those who may be going through a time of rebellion, are looking for an excuse to justify their behavior. The double standard or "hypocrisy" of their parents gives them that excuse. If you are a professing Christian, I must warn you that the most important place to live the Spirit-controlled life is in your home. That is where the Bible puts it!

Three passages in the New Testament command us to "walk in the [control of the] Spirit"—Galatians 5, Ephesians 5, and Colossians 3. As we have seen, the last two use the subject to introduce the lengthiest sections in the New Testament on family living. We must conclude, therefore, that God intended the Spirit-controlled life to be characterized by our conduct in the home. Quite clearly, if we can reflect that quality of life at home, we can reflect it anywhere! In fact, what we are at home is what we *really* are.

Our children know that—which is why they expect us to be imitators of Christ at home.

## Put on Virtues Like Clothes

The apostle Paul told the early Christians to "put off . . . anger, wrath, malice, slander," etc., and then added, "Put on . . ." a list of eight virtues. The words "put on" are translated in the NIV "clothe yourself." In other words, now that you are a Christian, just as you put on clothing when you get up in the morning, so "put on the proper clothing of Christian behavior." This clothing is identified in the NIV as "virtues." There are eight of them, seven in this chapter and a giant one in the next. As we consider them individually, we will find them ideal apparel for assuring a happy marriage adjustment, no matter how different the partners.

### 1. Put on compassion.

The initial trait in Colossians 3:12 is *compassion*. While compassion is similar to love, it primarily means "mercy" or "tenderness." Obviously it is much easier to live with a merciful person, sympathetic to the needs of others and filled with pity for others, than with one who is harsh and cruel.

All temperaments need compassion, but Cholerics require it more than others, greatly more than Phlegmatics and Melancholies. Of all the temperaments, the Sanguine has the easiest time showing "compassion" if he isn't too self-centered.

Twenty-seven years ago D.J. Dupree, owner and president of the second-largest furniture manufacturing company in the world and president of Christian Businessmen's International for five years, met the plane that my wife and I took to Grand Rapids, Michigan. Few men have impressed me more. He was 73 at the time and still dynamic, forceful, and well-organized, but he was also gracious and solicitous for our every need or desire. After our third day with him,

I told my wife, "When I am 73, I want to be that kind of man!"

Later I learned that he was not born that way. He bought the company during the Depression and, through dogged determination and hard work, built it into a very productive enterprise. Such forceful individuals are usually not gracious gentlemen. What changed him? The Spirit of God working through the Word of God in his life. Shortly after his conversion, which occurred in the late 1930s, he began to teach the Bible in his home. The Monday night Bible study grew to Tuesday and Thursday night studies. Today at least two churches, one in Zeeland and the other in Holland, Michigan, can be traced to those Bible studies. Not only were the people blessed, but so was the temperament of the teacher. "Compassion" was not a natural gift— it was supernatural. And it is available to any Christian who will seek it as a gift from God.

This trait (or virtue) is lacking in most people, particularly men. After my seminars, many men whose wives had left them often observe ruefully, "I wish I had heard this before; I drove my wife away by adopting the opposite approach." Never have I met a man who wore the garment of compassion and lost his wife. Women just don't leave that kind of man! The dream of every woman is to marry a man who loves her and shows that love by kindness. If given a choice between a good looking, well-to-do, forceful but somewhat cruel husband and a plain man who is compassionate, most women will opt for the latter every time.

## 2. Put on kindness.

The kindness that Paul challenges Christians to wear is not unique to him; it is a hallmark of Christianity, starting with our Lord Jesus and all the disciples. By nature human beings are not kind; it is a trait that must be learned. If you have traveled the world, you will find that wherever Christianity has gone, it has generated the state of kindness. It certainly is not consistently evident in the Orient, Africa, or India—except the Indian state of Karala, which traces its Christian roots to the first century, when Thomas the disciple brought the gospel to them.

Kindness, defined as the desire to do something good to other people, is the opposite of selfishness. Unselfish people are interested in being thoughtful and serving the needs of others. This becomes an invaluable tool for adjusting to one's opposite mate, for instead of looking for opportunities to take advantage of your partner, you are motivated to do good—even, as our Lord challenged us, "when they despitefully use us."

A Christian man I met in India was obviously loved by his wife of many years, even though that is a land where such emotions are not publicly displayed. When I mentioned it to him, he surprised me by declaring, "It was not always that way." Their parents had arranged the marriage at a time when she really had her heart set on another man. But in India a woman has little choice in such matters. Being committed to the work of the Lord, he realized that he must *win* his wife's affection; he could not demand it. For several weeks he disciplined himself on sexual expression but continually treated her kindly. She had received little kindness in her life from her father, and in a few weeks her husband wooed her into consummating their wedding vows. Obviously her love had continued to grow with the passing years. It is a rare woman who does not respond to kindness.

No temperament seems naturally disposed to benevolence. Sanguines bestow it to gain approval or friendship. Melancholies offer it when they are in the right mood, and Phlegmatics only do it under compulsion. Cholerics look on kindness as an act of weakness. Whenever you see a kind, thoughtful person continually trying to serve others, you are looking at a miracle of God, a Christian who walks in the control of the Spirit.

*3. Put on humility.*

The challenge to be humble is unique to Christianity. In fact, most other cultures ascribe little or no value to it. The Greeks, like modern-day secular humanists, esteemed high-minded self-sufficiency and self-seeking. In the Western world, the philosopher Nietzsche castigated the humble as though their very existence promoted feelings of inferiority. It certainly was contrary to his commitment to the superiority of certain races.

The Bible, however, upholds humility as a virtue that demonstrates our total dependence on God. Frequently mentioned as a virtue by the wise man of Proverbs, it was best exemplified by our Lord when He made Himself lower than the angels so that He could taste death for every man. We as individual Christians are challenged to imitate His humility by the words, "Let this mind be in you that was in Christ Jesus." Nothing more readily demonstrates that we are walking in carnality and self-will and not the Holy Spirit than the absence of humility.

All temperaments have a problem with natural humility. Sanguines are prone to be arrogant and self-inflated. Cholerics tend toward pride—the exact opposite of humility—and Melancholies by nature can be self-righteous and critical of others—like Cholerics, totally intolerant of the weaknesses of others. Phlegmatics may seem to be humble because they are quiet and passive, but often while they sit on the outside of the group, they are really standing up in pride on the inside. They may not be as obnoxious as their more extrovertish friends, but they have fought battles in the arena of pride.

The Christian who denies that he faces a lifetime struggle with pride is not telling the truth. And remember, just when we seek the Lord for the gift of humility and see His power demonstrated in our life, we are apt to get puffed up with pride. Satan demonstrated that sin begins with pride, and has tempted every person since Eve with that same sin.

True humility emanates from our relationship to God. The further a person is from God, the more inclined he is to be proud; the closer he is to God, the more apt he is to don the robe of humility. Why have God's most humble servants enjoyed a lifetime pattern of daily Bible study and prayer? Because they really understood the challenge, "Without me you can do nothing." This total dependency on God forced them to be consistent in the Word and prayer.

Humility can be obtained whatever one's temperament. Pride makes us self-dependent, whereas humility impels us to be "others-conscious." The Bible promises, "Humble yourself under the mighty hand of God and He will exalt you."

A man entered the counseling room one day with his wife and forthrightly announced, "Preacher, there is no hope for this marriage!" This man, the father of four sons, repeated the statement three times and for emphasis pounded his fist on the table each time. Three hours later, when we had come to an impasse and I really saw no hope for them, I silently prayed, "Lord, I have done everything I know to do and said everything I know to say, but nothing has worked. If this marriage is to be saved, You will have to perform a miracle." Even I was amazed when in a matter of moments the man burst into tears and dropped to his knees, recommitting his life to Christ. When he finally stopped crying, he stood up, hugged his wife, and completely reversed his position. At the outset of the interview he had reproached her for the unhappiness in their marriage. When he humbled himself before God, he immediately accepted all the blame and asked her to forgive him.

He hasn't been perfect since then, but after seven years they still have a Christ-honoring and happy marriage. It all started with humility, which is an attitude of heart—the mental attitude that says, "Lord, in my flesh dwells no good thing . . . without You I can do nothing!" Humble couples do not have indissoluble differences, regardless of temperament conflicts.

### 4. Put on gentleness.

Gentleness is so similar to humility that they are often used together in the Scriptures—and they are the two virtues least desired by the pagan world of ancient times or even by humanists today. Oh, many people like to see meekness in others, but they have little desire to establish the trait in themselves.

Our Lord, of course, exemplified true gentleness (as He did all the traits He demands of us). In Matthew 11:29 He said, "Take my yoke upon you and learn from me, for I am gentle and humble in heart, and you will find rest for your souls" (NIV). You may be more familiar with the King James Version of that verse, which says, "I am meek and lowly in heart." In the two translations we may equate "gentle" with meek and "humble" with lowly in heart.

In the beatitudes our Lord promised, "Happy are the gentle [meek] in heart, for they will inherit the earth." Those who are meek enough to humble themselves and become themselves dependent on God are the ones to whom He will entrust the earth in the next life. Any student of history will testify that the study of man is primarily a history of war because the countries of this world have never been run by the gentle or meek but by the proud and greedy self-seekers. But the same is true of factious families and partners. Gentle spirits do not clash!

Of all the temperaments, only the Phlegmatic seems gentle by nature because any mean-spiritedness he might feel will be manifested diplomatically and subtly. Sanguines are the opposite of "gentle"; they are like the proverbial "bull in the china shop," too self-centered to be meek. Cholerics view meekness as a sign of weakness, and thus Christianity may seem too passive and impotent for them. The

Melancholy's lack of meekness is often demonstrated by his compulsion to criticize and correct others. All temperaments need help in learning gentleness, but once the lesson has been mastered it becomes a great healer to fragile relationships.

Gentleness has been described as "the opposite of arrogance and self-assertiveness, the special mark of the man who has a delicate consideration for the rights and feelings of others." But it seems an unnatural trait, so it must be supplied by the Spirit of God. That is why it is listed as one of the fruits of the Spirit.

A very sensitive woman married to an extremely callous man had attempted divorce three times after years of frigidity and unhappiness. Only their three children had kept them together. One of the major deterrents to a good sex life (besides their anger, which both seemed well-equipped to manifest) was his lovemaking vocabulary. Having been in the military service, he knew every vulgar word for all parts of the human anatomy. To him that was "common speech." To her the terminology was offensive. "Those words turn me off!" she protested. After they had prayerfully recommitted their lives and marriage to the Lord, he tenderly said, "Honey, I'm sorry I have offended you all these years. With God's help I will never use that kind of gutter language again. If I do, I will ask your pardon." Now that is gentleness—a willingness to conform our behavior, even our speech patterns, to another person's preferences.

Gentleness is not self-seeking; it is more interested in fulfilling the needs of others than one's self. When you seek God's help to change your preferences to those of your partner, in the long run you benefit more than he does. According to our Lord, "Whatever a person sows, he reaps." But we always reap more than we sow; that is a divine principle. Sow a grain of corn and you grow at least one whole ear with many grains. Sow gentleness and you reap a harvest of soothing, kindly feelings.

When Bev and I found that we were total cultural mismatches, her gentle spirit saved the day. She loves classical music, whereas I can live without it. She is eager to attend concerts, symphonies, and plays; I prefer sports events, though I only allow myself to be a one-sport fan, for otherwise sports would consume me. I chose football because it is my favorite sport and occupies only five months a year.

After a few weeks of marriage I discovered that Bev was not enthusiastic about football. About the same time she discovered the serious deficiency in my cultural appreciation. When I asked why she wouldn't attend football games with me, she claimed not to "understand football," and I had to admit that I was no aficionado of music! So we had a decision to make: Would we go our separate ways for hobbies, or could we work out a compromise? After discussing it at length, we settled on the plan that she would attend nine football games with me each year and I would take her to one concert. Frankly, I thought she was getting the best of the bargain.

When we moved to San Diego, we turned from college to professional football, and for three years I taught the Chargers Bible study in our home. Now we were combining sports and ministry. In addition, we discovered that Charger halftimes featured a band concert, so Bev was now the recipient of one main concert and nine miniconcerts each year. Then one day while attending a game, she asked me to explain why I always became so tense on "third-down plays." For the first time I realized that she didn't understand the significance of that play, the key to understanding the game. She is a quick learner, so within a game or two football became an exciting event for her, and today she is as avid a Redskins fan as I am. Often when I am traveling to a seminar during game time, I call home while waiting for my next plane, and she provides an update on the game in progress.

It is no longer a sacrifice for her to give me nine games, which she thoroughly enjoys so she can drag me to one concert. When we lived in Washington, D.C., we were just a few blocks from the Kennedy Center for the Performing Arts, which features some of the finest programs in the world, I would take her to three or more concerts a year— and our son would accompany her to four or five more. Our present harmony started in college, when Bev was willing to meekly or gently give more than she received. Now she receives more than she must give.

When we put on the virtue of gentleness, we are obeying the Lord—and making a giant step toward adjusting to our opposite partner.

## 5. *Put on patience.*

This fifth virtue appears many times in Scripture. Often it is used in reference to God; several times it is exemplified in our Lord when He was on this earth. We as Christians are to "put it on," which suggests that it is not a staple part of the Christian's wardrobe. Patience, which means "longsuffering," has been described as "that calm and unruffled temper with which the good man bears the evils of life, whether they proceed from things or people."

Patience cheerfully anticipates a better day when the tribulations of life strike us. We can only receive it through the Spirit-filled life and the exercise of faith, which is built up during times of trial. James 1:2,3 indicates that we manifest patience when we project joy, by faith, even in the face of adversity.

Every marriage endures difficult times; all human relationships undergo stress. If we confront these times patiently, we do not scar relationships. But if we react in the flesh, our differences will be accentuated.

Patience is one of the clear evidences of love. When we send out love signals, patience naturally accompanies them. But when we love ourselves more than someone else, impatience just as naturally arises. Four sons of a woman Bible teacher entered the ministry in spite of the fact that her husband was a hopeless alcoholic who literally drank himself to death. They had seen her patiently wait on her drunken husband, wash him when he was in a filthy stupor, nurse him back to health after he incurred self-inflicted sicknesses, and finally bury him after he drank himself into a premature grave. One of them pronounced his mother "a saint." She was a strong woman, not patient by nature. But she never treated her husband contemptuously because of his weakness, and her sons discerned their Savior in the way she patiently treated their father.

Sanguines and Cholerics are usually very impatient. Forever in a hurry and quick on the lip, they will devastate others verbally when a few seconds of patience would have kept them from wielding their tongue like a warrior's sword to inflict maximum damage. Whenever you meet a patient extrovert, you are viewing Spirit-filled temperament in human shoe leather. Melancholies are far more patient than the two just mentioned, but their tendency to criticism, revenge, and other negative thinking patterns makes them far less patient than they should be.

Phlegmatics can be patient and kind in the midst of cruelty, but their motivation may originate in fear and self-protection rather than love or concern for someone else. And if they should cross the line of patience, it is most difficult to get them to try again. A carnal Christian woman who knew nothing about the Spirit-controlled life endured 25 years of a bad marriage before finally kicking her husband out of the house. Once she did so, however, I was afraid it would take another 25 years to readmit him. Only when she was willing to submit her stubborn will to God and give her repentant husband another chance could she salvage her marriage. Today she is glad she did. But Phlegmatics generally seem to have the greatest difficulty recrossing the line once their patience has snapped.

*6. Put on forbearance.*

Americans know little about forbearance, which is a virtue unique to Christianity. It literally means putting up graciously and patiently with someone else's weakness when it counters the area of your strength. We have already examined this in relation to the adjustment stage of marriage. Once we see our partners as they really are—including weaknesses—we are apt to lose our love for them, to treat them with criticism, contempt, and other forms of disapproval. A constant fixation on weakness will kill the strongest love and in many cases even the sex drive.

Whenever that happens, we must concede that the Christian has not been led of the Spirit but has dealt with the exposure of weakness in the flesh—as if he were not a Christian. Now is the time to "put on forbearance" and love your spouse anyway.

"Forbearance" is used in the Bible primarily to describe the way God looked on us while we were yet sinners: He loved us anyway. And that is what the Christian is expected to do: Never allowing weaknesses to impair love, we must overlook the problem and treat the partner gently, with patience and mercy. Forbearance can put new life and sparkle into any marriage. It is the glue that God has given to insure long and happy marriages. Relationships without forbearance usually don't last long—and if they do, happiness is never paramount.

*7. Put on forgiveness.*

One characteristic of long, pleasure-filled marriages is forgiveness. Cholerics and Melancholies have the greatest difficulty with intolerance. Cholerics are famous for allowing only one strike in their ball game, which makes it difficult for them to forgive. Melancholies may pardon, but an intolerant spirit and incredible memory for negative feelings causes them to recall injuries again and again. Of all the temperaments, Sanguines find it most easy to forgive. "No one's perfect," they cheerfully observe, "so don't worry about it."

As we have already noted, all relationships need forgiveness. Any couple, even those with the best marriages, have had to learn to forgive. I will not belabor the point again except to add that even though forgiveness may be extremely difficult for you, if you refuse to forgive when necessary, it carries a severe price—spiritually, emotionally, physically, and relationally.

Failing to forgive will hurt you spiritually because the anger that accompanies it grieves the Holy Spirit (Ephesians 4:30-32) and hinders your prayer life (1 Peter 3:7). In addition, our Lord made it clear that if we do not forgive others their trespasses, He will not forgive ours (Matthew 6:14,15). No one will advance spiritually until he learns to "put on forgiveness." A spirit of animosity is expensive physically because it can trigger numerous diseases. Emotionally it creates harmful feelings and stifles the flow of love, joy, and peace. Relationally it creates stony hearts and steel wills, which all too frequently direct the marriage into the divorce court—and then the acrimony and recriminations that follow will further damage children even after their home has been torn apart.

Forgiveness is not optional; it is the will of God, His mandate for all Christians. Millions of marriages today can trace their present harmony to a point of forgiveness by one or both partners. Recently I dealt with a Christian couple in which both had been unfaithful—the husband out of lust and deceit, the wife in retaliation. There was seemingly no hope for this couple until they sincerely sought the forgiveness of God. Once they accepted divine absolution, they solicited His help to forgive their mate. It is too early to make a final judgment, but I suspect that their relationship will heal.

Many years ago, when a woman in our church confronted her husband with evidence of adultery, he admitted his sin and sincerely repented. After she forgave him, they were reconciled. Three months later she was back in my office. "I have lost all feeling for my husband. I just can't stand to have him touch me!" I confronted her with the fact that she had not really forgiven him, and thus her feeling for him had died. Angrily she responded, "Why should I forgive him? He doesn't deserve it. He knew better than that! We were both raised in the same church, and he knew adultery was a sin." I sympathized with her distress, but her lack of forgiveness was protracting the pain. So I asked, "Do you want to be miserable or happy the rest of your life?" She tearfully responded, "I want to be happy, of course." "Then you will have to forgive him as the Bible commands—not as he deserves to be forgiven, but as God in Christ Jesus forgave you."

## You Don't Have to Be Perfect

There you have seven of the eight pieces of the Christian's wardrobe. How many have you "put on"? Your answer provides a good test of your happiness in marriage. If you are wearing 60 percent, I suspect you are enjoying 60 percent of the happiness God has for you. It's time to don more of your Christian apparel—by "walking in the Spirit." By this time you have probably noticed that the "walk in the Spirit" command of Galatians 5:16-23 is almost identical to "putting on" the apparel of the Christian in Colossians 3. The final garment is like a topcoat, the one that covers all the rest.

# *Communicate Your Love*

> Now these three remain: faith, hope and love, but the greatest of these is love (1 Corinthians 13:13 NIV).

> Over all these virtues, put on love, which binds them all together in perfect unity (Colossians 3:14 NIV).

The Bible has a great deal to say about love. We learn that "God is love" and that "if we love God . . . we will love one another." By contrast, if we hate our brother, it is a sign that the love of God is not in us.

The Bible also enjoins us to love our mate. Husbands are commanded four times to love their wives. Wives should love their husband and children and be keepers of the home (Titus 2:4,5).

God expects Christian couples to manifest true love for a lifetime. Isn't that why we get married in the first place? One evidence that we fully love God is that we love one another. The Christian couple united in love is a graphic testimony to the love of God working in them. I have already shared Emerson's quote, "Love is an emotion that ends with marriage." That sums up the attitude of worldly people toward this incredible emotion, largely because they try to do it in their own strength, forgetting that sinful man always falls short of the standards of God. But with God's help, love can grow with each passing year so that a couple can truly say, "I love you more today than when we were married."

## Everyone Needs Love

Mankind universally needs to love and be loved. For this reason millions of people every year relinquish their independence to be "yoked together." This becomes the most important relationship in life, as underscored by the fact that fully 75 percent of those who divorce because the first marriage did not produce enduring love try it again. Almost 50 percent of those second marriages fail, but the attempt to renew a marital relationship after failure suggests that human beings have an instinctual desire to share their life with another member of the opposite sex. That this demands personal and financial sacrifice does not deter us; we are driven by a need to love and be loved.

The most devastating experience on earth is to be rejected by the person you love. Whether another person, drugs, alcohol, or even work, rejection is a demoralizing and sometimes debilitating experience. Most people don't realize that a large percent of those who are spurned lose their mate because they did not administer love.

A brilliant engineer and father of five paced up and down in front of my desk, obviously in great anguish over the fact that his wife had left him and their children to run off with a sailor whose income was only one-fourth as large as his. He diagnosed his own problem when I asked, "Did you communicate to your wife that you loved her?" "Maybe that was my problem. She was always after me to tell her I loved her, but I never would. I preferred to prove my love. I gave her a second car when she wanted it and I just bought new carpeting for our home." Demonstrating the typical male intelligence, he added, "I gave her five children, didn't I?" Upon questioning, he admitted he had not verbalized his love for ten years. Yet he claimed to be in love.

The sailor, by contrast, had nothing to give the woman but his love. She was so love-starved that she decided to sacrifice everything to get it—for a time. Usually such women live to regret that decision. The affair is of brief duration, and then she is again unloved, but now without her children. I am convinced that she would never have found the sailor attractive had her husband been willing to communicate his love in terms that she would comprehend.

Most men don't understand women and thus treat them as they themselves like to be treated. This man did not need to hear his wife say "I love you!"—at least not at the stage of his life when self-acceptance was coming largely from his vocational success. But his wife did need to hear those words; most women do. It is a natural part of an intimate relationship, which is why God commanded men to "love your wife." Women need love, and men must be reminded to communicate it in terms their wife can understand.

Men often scheme to buy their wife's affection with "a second car," "new carpeting," or "diamonds." Most men could save themselves a major outlay of funds if they would just say, "Honey, I love you and would still select you if I had the choice to make all over again." A woman finds that assuring, particularly when such statements are reinforced with the right kind of treatment. Several years ago, *USA TODAY* published the results of a survey on marriage that is most revealing. When asked the question, "If you had the chance to make the choice all over again, would you marry the same woman?" Seventy-two percent of the married men said yes, while 51 percent of the married women responded no! Then the survey addressed the same question to women who had answered positively to the previous question, "Does your husband volunteer to help out around the house?" Eighty-two percent of those who received such voluntary indications of love and respect were affirmative. They would marry the same man all over again.

Women don't want men to be household slaves; they simply crave love, communicated both verbally and physically. I seem to make real brownie points with my wife when I voluntarily head for the dishwasher and put away the clean dishes. For some reason she doesn't like that job. She fills the dishwasher with dirty dishes as soon as a meal is finished, but for some reason she drags her feet when it comes to putting them away. I find myself reaching into the dishwasher, not because the task is enjoyable but because she appreciates the gesture—and I love to make her happy.

The same is true with vacuuming. The arthritis in Bev's shoulders make the process difficult, so I do it myself. When the machine roars into action before she even asks, you would think I had just bought her a dozen roses! (At the price of roses today, my time must be worth 20 dollars an hour, but the reaction I get is far more valuable!)

A wise partner looks for opportunities to please his wife. That isn't weakness; it is love. Much like electricity, we can't see love, but we can certainly judge its presence by what it does.

When I was a very young minister, I watched the effect of love in marriage as a result of two back-to-back counseling experiences. I drove to Lake Minnetonka by request to counsel a very rich couple. They had everything—a beautiful boat at the dock, two big cars in the garage, and a palatial home with carpet so deep that I almost sank in it to my knees. Love, however, was nowhere to be found, because the icicles of anger permeated their home. I was unable to help them, and they ended up in a divorce after a long and bitter battle over their "things."

The next morning I drove up a muddy road to the poorest family in the church. They had three daughters, and their son was just going into the service. They had asked me to come and pray for this young man and their home. They had only six chairs in the kitchen, so they turned an orange crate on edge for me to sit on as I sipped coffee at the breakfast table. As we talked, I watched the looks of love and comments of endearment pass between this husband and wife of at least 24 years. They were so poor that she never went to a beauty parlor, always wore the same nice outfit to church, and sewed all the girls' clothes—yet she loved the man who had only love to bestow upon her. It dawned on me that love is the most affordable commodity in life.

Always express love in terms that communicate to your partner. Sanguine, Phlegmatic, and Melancholy partners need verbal expressions of love. But the Melancholy will watch your actions carefully to make sure they match your speech. Cholerics pretend they don't need to be reassured, although secretly they do. They tend to measure your love, however, by your productivity. A hot meal when he opens the door is often better than love notes. Melancholies are incurable romantics: They love candles, notes, perfumes, music, and incredible amounts of time, all saying in terms they can understand, "I love you!"

## Super Love Equals Super Sex

A vital marriage includes mutual sexual satisfaction. That is the way God designed our anatomy, minds, feelings, and even our hormones. But men and women are different, and these contrasts are compounded by both their sex and their opposite temperaments.

To men, sex is an experience. To women, it is a process. If couples, particularly husbands, do not understand that fact, they never develop the love life of which they are capable. According to the Bible, love "does not seek its own," meaning its own satisfaction. All couples, no matter how loving, must accommodate each other sexually on some occasions. Admittedly, at certain special times both are in the mood, the conditions are just right, and they enjoy super sex. But what about the days when one is interested and the other is not? At that juncture 1 Corinthians 7:1-5 must be practiced. As a married person, your body is no longer your exclusive property; it also belongs to your mate. If you love your partner as Christ loved the church, you will adjust to the needs of your partner rather than yourself, whenever possible.

Married women regularly complain, "Whenever I get near my husband, the only thing he thinks about is sex. I need time to get into the mood." Some temperaments require more time than others, but as a general rule, women like a long, romantic buildup, whereas men are ready to go at a moment's notice. When a man understands this, if he loves his wife, he will adapt his quick-start passions to her slow-burn response. Many nonsexual but affectionate touches should precede what I like to call "the act of marriage." The wife who has been romanced and affectionately treated during the evening is usually interested in culminating the evening with what my doctor friend Ed Wheat, who has written extensively on this subject, calls "enjoying each other physically." That's super sex, prompted by super love.

The "joys of sex" are heralded broadly today—championed mostly by men who don't understand the differences between men and women in this area. They make it seem that super sex leads to super love when in reality it is just the opposite. Super sex is eagerly enjoyed by a partner to whom is granted super love. And remember, super love generates many unselfish expressions of love, from denying yourself to joyfully meeting the needs of your partner.

## Be Creative!

One characteristic of love as described in 1 Corinthians 13 is thoughtfulness. The most thoughtful gestures may be quite meaningless to you but filled with significance to your partner, particularly if he knows you are primarily endeavoring to please him.

Several years ago while on a mission trip to Europe, I was jogging in the hotel section of Vienna, Austria. The huge building I was passing was dark and ugly from the outside, but the sign read "Stodt Opera House." At first it meant nothing to me, but then I recognized it as one of the most famous opera houses in Europe. Inside I discovered that it was featuring the final showing of Don Giovanni. I bought two good seats, rushed back to the hotel, and announced, "Get gussied up, Bev. I'm taking you out tonight." We had a romantic dinner and then walked to the Opera House. I thought she would leap out of her skin! Very honestly, watching the troupe prancing around in leotards, singing Italian, did not inspire me. But watching Bev thoroughly enjoy herself did. She suspected that I was enduring a form of torture, but she recognized that it represented the sacrifice of love. And she has never forgotten that memorable moment, which was a hundred times more effective than usual because I thought of it myself (though quite by accident). Find those areas that are meaningful to your mate and use them to express your love.

An engineer in Pasadena, a collector and restorer of old classic cars, merits "the most creative expression of love" award. One day he announced that he would need the family car for a four-day solo business trip to San Francisco. After two days his beautiful Sanguine wife had become a bit "stir crazy" and thought of an excuse to get out of the house and go to the store. The only vehicle available was the 1958 classic, two-seat Thunderbird convertible her husband had completely restored. He had taken everything on that car apart, cleaned it, and put it back together. With his new high-gloss paint job, it actually looked better than when it rolled off the assembly line. It was his pride and joy.

The young wife went to the garage and pulled back the tarp under which he always kept it. "Wow," she thought, "would I like to drive that!" After a moment she reflected, "Charlie never said I couldn't drive it," so she started it up and proceeded down the street. Can you picture this free-spirited woman with a long ponytail blowing freely as she sped down the road? Everything went well until suddenly a panel truck came out of nowhere and totaled her husband's car. She was not injured, but she did lament, "My husband will kill me for wrecking his car!" When the police officer asked for the customary identification, they finally located the registration in the glove compartment. It was in a clear plastic packet that testified to her husband's temperament. With it was the owner's manual and the record of every expenditure, including gas, oil, and mileage at each oil change. Then she noticed an envelope with her name on it. This is what she read:

> Dear Beth:
>
> If you are reading this note, it is because you have had an accident with my car. Just remember, honey—I love you most of all!
>
> Charlie

Now that is love creativity at its best!

## Love Is a Decision

Gary Smalley and John Trent are popular family seminar teachers out of Phoenix, Arizona. While watching a Christian TV station one night, I spotted the advertisement of their seminar called "Love Is a Decision." I was quite impressed with what I saw and agree that love involves decision-making. This has always been true, even when arranged marriages brought two almost-total strangers together for a lifetime. They either made up their mind to love each other or determined to "tough it out together." In either case, it was a matter of the will.

God has commanded us many times in the Bible to "love one another." If two married Christians cannot love, they are two people out of the will of God. If they protest, "I just can't love that person," they are right. Love (or the lack of love) is based on a decision. If, however, they pledge, "With God's help I will love you," they open the door to a whole new way of life emotionally. No one can force you to love; that is between you and the Lord. Remember this, however: God never commands us to do what He will not enable us to do.

In the previous chapter we reviewed the seven pieces of apparel that we are to "put on" now that we have become Christians. This eighth one, found in verse 14 of Colossians 3, deserves a complete chapter. Consider these words: "Above all these things put on love, which is the bond of perfection." The NIV more accurately translates it ". . . which binds them all together in perfect unity."

In this context, love is the outer garment—the most critical of all. We put it on after everything else is in place. When the finishing garment of love overlays the rest, all else remains intact. When we take it off, other parts of our garment may begin to unravel. This outer garment of love, which "covers a multitude of sins," is the greatest gift we can give to another person.

## How to Keep Your Love Alive

Briggs and Alice Olson had loved each other for over 50 years. She was the organist in our first full-time church in Minneapolis; he was chairman of the building committee and trustee board. They were like adoptive parents to my wife and me. We were young, fresh out of college in our first church, and they were our closest neighbors. The first thing we noticed about them was their great love for each other. Since then we have observed many loving couples, but none more devoted than this one.

In watching truly loving couples through the years, I have noticed that they all seem to possess four characteristics in common. These could be identified as "the keys to keeping your love alive."

*1. They were Spirit-filled Christians most of the time.*

Oh, they weren't perfect—no one is. But they wanted to walk in the Spirit on a daily basis, knowing that the first fruit of the Spirit is love. One cannot walk in the Spirit and fail to love his partner!

*2. They were kind, thoughtful, and respectful partners.*

I never heard Briggs or Alice, who are now in heaven, say a cross word to each other. Rather than putting each other down, they pumped each other up. Modern psychologists call it "stroking." They didn't know what it was called—they just did it. Whenever you were with them, you had the feeling that you were always welcome, but when you left them, you knew that they were just as happy being alone together. That reflects a healthy marriage.

*3. They didn't dwell on anything negative.*

Neither was perfect—they were quick to admit that—but whenever they talked about the past, it was always in the positive. The regrettable, unfortunate events were rarely if ever brought up.

*4. They openly thanked God for bringing them together and for their cheerful, productive life.*

I have noticed that thankful people are happy people, and happy people are easier to love.

## How to Reignite Sputtering Love

In this fast-paced modern age, many couples wake up one day to discover that they are no longer sweethearts. In fact, they may even be getting tired of each other. As some couples describe it, "Our love has died."

Through the years I have developed a simple formula for reigniting that love. It works no matter how dead the love seems at first. Remember, "With man this is impossible for you, but with God, nothing is impossible for you!" I simply ask the couple to incorporate all four of the above steps and then add one more . . .

*5. Make a list of ten things about your partner that you like.*

Thank God twice every day for those ten things, and do not ponder their negative traits. Love will automatically follow a thankful heart. And 1 Thessalonians 5:18 clearly verifies that this kind of thanksgiving living "is the will of God in Christ Jesus concerning you."

A businessman invited me down to his posh club for lunch and spent 25 minutes rehearsing every negative characteristic of his wife. He ended by saying, "We are in serious trouble! We no longer love each other and have lost all feeling for each other. We have not slept in the same bedroom in three months. If we weren't Christians and had a son to raise, we would get a divorce."

Ignoring his outburst, I asked, "How would you like to fall madly in love with your wife within a three-week span of time?" He glared at me skeptically, but the possibility intrigued him. "Is that possible?" he asked. "Yes, I have developed a formula that I know will work. If you follow it faithfully, the two of you can be happier than you have ever been before."

Taking a three-by-five card out of my pocket, I asked him to name something about his wife that he liked. He thought for 15 minutes and finally announced, "My wife is good to my mother!" Then I asked for another thing, and before long we had filled the card with a list of ten items that he had begrudgingly provided.

Handing the card to him, I challenged him to thank God twice daily for those ten things—in the morning during his quiet time and as he drove home from work each night. In addition, every time he thought of something critical, he was to replace it with a thanksgiving item from the list.

Ten days went by. On Sunday night they attended evening service—which was not common for them—and came up to talk for a moment afterward. As we chatted, he put his arm around his wife's shoulder and she cuddled up to him. I was impressed. Sometimes body language is an outstanding disseminator of truth. By the time we finished talking, the church was empty and they started to leave. As she preceded him through the swinging double doors, he lagged back long enough to murmur in a stage whisper, "We're back in the same bedroom together!" That definitely showed progress. Three weeks to the day, I called him from the San Diego airport on church business and concluded by asking, "How are things coming along at home?" I thought for a minute he would melt and come right through the phone! He began to expound upon the joys of marriage and the bliss of their love relationship.

I must admit that I immediately became somewhat carnal. I wanted to know if my little card system was responsible for their incredible progress, but I hesitated to ask him directly. So I inquired, "Do you have those ten items on that card memorized yet?" I will never forget his response. "Oh, yes! I had them memorized by the third day, but I turned your card over and added 15 other things that I like about her."

Evidently thanksgiving produces more thanksgiving, and that engenders love. Try it; you'll like it!

> Over all these virtues put on LOVE, which binds them all together in perfect unity (Colossians 3:14 NIV).

Everyone craves love! But most people solicit it from others, which is not the way to get it! The Bible says, "Give and it will be given to you: good measure, pressed down, shaken together, and running over will be put into your bosom. For with the same measure that you use, it will be measured back to you" (Luke 6:38).

Obviously from that verse we learn that if we want love, we are to give it. And with the same measure we give, it will be measured out to us.

Incidentally, when it comes to imparting love, use a big scoop. Then prepare to reap a rich harvest of love. That's God's law.

## Give Your Love a Test

Selfishness is such a subtle foe that most people find it all but impossible to be objective about their love. We need to replace "Do I love him or her?" with "Do I love him more than I love myself?" Only that measures true love. The test on the following page will give you an opportunity to scrutinize your love. Give yourself a fair and objective score from zero to ten on each question and then total your points.

If you scored 90 or above, you have an ideal love; keep cultivating it. If you scored in the low 80s, begin to apply the principles in this second half of the book to your life and marriage. If your score dipped into the low 70s, your relationship is in decline; talk to your pastor or a Christian counselor. Anyone who scores in the low 60s will be rather unhappy with his mate. You are in trouble, and the situation will not improve without outside help. Run, don't walk, to your church for counsel and support.

The key to all relationships is quite simple: Put on love! With God's help you can do it.

## *The Ten-Point Love Test*

1. \_\_\_\_ Do you have a strong and affectionate bond of caring about your mate's needs and desires that inspires a willingness on your part to sacrifice to fulfill him?

2. \_\_\_\_ Do you enjoy your partner's personality, companionship, and friendship?

3. \_\_\_\_ Do you share common goals and interests which you communicate freely?

4. \_\_\_\_ Do you respect and admire your mate in spite of recognized needs or weaknesses in his/her life, or even when you disagree with decisions?

5. \_\_\_\_ Do you have a unique sexual attraction for each other that leads frequently to mutually satisfactory expressions of the act of marriage?

6. \_\_\_\_ Do you desire children (if physically possible) who share both of your physical and temperament characteristics and to whom you can impart your moral and spiritual values (or did you when you were the appropriate age)?

7. \_\_\_\_ Do you share a vital faith in God that is a helpful influence on each other spiritually?

8. \_\_\_\_ Do you have a sense of permanence and possession about your mate to such a degree that others of the opposite sex are not similarly attractive to you?

9. \_\_\_\_ Do you have a growing desire to spend more time with your partner?

10. \_\_\_\_ Do you have a genuine appreciation for your partner's individual successes?

_____ **Total Score**

# *How to Become Best Friends*

> Loneliness is the first thing which God named not good. . . . There is a peculiar comfort in the marriage state beside the genial bed, which no other society affords. . . . If conditions (of companionship) be not fulfilled, there is no real marriage (John Milton, 1643).

After a Family Life Seminar where Dr. Henry Brandt and I were speaking, a couple came to us and asked, "Dr. Brandt, what advice would you give a couple whose last child is a senior in high school and will only be living in our home another six months?" Without a moment's hesitation he replied, "You had better become each other's best friend."

That is doubtless what John Milton, the great seventeenth-century writer, meant in his tract *The Doctrine and Discipline of Divorce*, as quoted above. He further stated,

> In God's intention, a meet and happy conversation is the chiefest and noblest end of marriage. . . . The chief society thereof is in the soul rather than in the body, and the greatest breach thereof is unfitness of mind rather than defect of body . . . since we know that it is not the joining of another body that will

remove loneliness but the uniting of another com-
pliable mind.

In spite of the old English style, it is clear that both John
Milton and Henry Brandt put the highest priority in marriage on two people becoming each other's best friend.

Quite honestly, most couples who marry hardly even
know the person with whom they will spend the rest of their
life. They think they do, but they are so caught up with
interchanging waves of libido, which is strongest between
the ages of 17 and 24 (when most people marry, or at least
used to until promiscuity became so rampant), that they
only sustain a surface friendship. Not until their sex drives
(the Bible calls it "burning") are satisfied in the act of marriage do they begin to really get acquainted with each
other. In every marriage there are surprises, some good and
some bad. The surprises start with the selfishness quotient,
the anger or the fears, and then habits, tastes, and temperament differences, just to name a few that we have
already examined.

Most couples will probably not become "best friends"
for several years after they marry. They need time to know,
appreciate, and like each other, and only a passage of time
permits them to invest in one another, beginning with children, home, vocation, and interests. I have watched couples who were on the verge of divorce and thought they
were worst enemies learn to become best friends. Those
who have never tried to examine the art of friendship
inevitably succumb to the alternative—a miserable, lonely
life. Marriage should solve loneliness, which is why God
gave Eve to Adam.

Unfortunately, union with a partner does not always
resolve an individual's loneliness; instead, it can lock the
person into a relationship from which he cannot escape. If
partners do not learn to become true friends, their marriage turns into a solitary existence. God never intended

that. He designed marriage to produce the best friendship two people could share on this earth. If, however, it has not automatically happened to you, don't despair; friendship can be learned. I include this chapter in the hope that those who are committed for life but realize they are not as close as two people can and should be will gain insights they can incorporate into their marriage and soon become each other's best friend.

## People Change

People change during the long years of marriage. One hundred years ago, when the mortality rate was 34 years for men and 37 years for women, that wasn't so important—and it may be one reason why divorce was not so common then. An individual just did not live so long that the passage of years made him seem like "another person." Now, however, the mortality rate is 73 years for men and 77 years for women; consequently we spend much more of our life married. That frequently permits such changes that after the children are gone, married partners are like two strangers living in the same household.

## The Marks of a Best Friend

Marriage is not the only friendship we experience in life. Most of us had best friends with whom we grew up or attended church or school, and our friendships flourished because we shared many things in common. It was, however, an asexual friendship that was replaced by a superior relationship when we married. Gradually that other same-sex friendship began to fade as we learned the joys of a marital relationship and invested ourselves in common interests. Couples can maintain couple friendships and individual friendships after marriage (people with whom we spend time and in whom we can confide at pressure spots in our lives), but marriage can maintain only one opposite-sex best friend.

A couple does not have to agree on everything or be interested only in areas of common interest to be good friends, but they must develop sufficient areas of interest to enjoy being together most of the time. Neither party should be threatened when one goes with friends on a retreat, hunting trip, or sporting activity, for periods of brief separation can make them appreciate each other even more. But close friends basically enjoy spending time together.

The statements by John Milton utilize the word "companionship" much as we use the term "friendship." Best friends are really best companions—a relationship which is well worth the effort to preserve.

## The Characteristics of a Best Friend

People seldom set out to become best friends; the bonding just happens. Sometimes opposite temperaments draw them together, and then certain commonalities develop a resilient friendship. Such a relationship, unlike marriage, can last for years because it is not overexposed by a 24-hour-a-day surveillance. For even though a married couple is drawn together through many common areas of interest, their differences can become overpowering—particularly if selfishness, anger, or fear are not brought under control. I am not sure it is possible for a person to become best friends with a selfish, angry, or fear-dominated spouse. Under such circumstances the negative often becomes so dominant in the mind of the partner that he can no longer appreciate the positive trait. Most of the following characteristics will be found in a solid friendship:

1. Someone you enjoy being with.

2. Someone with whom you share many interests.

3. Someone with whom you can communicate freely.

4. Someone in whom you can confide, and who will never betray you.

5. Someone about whose interests and well-being you genuinely care.

6. Someone whose faults you overlook.

7. Someone with whom you can laugh, cry, and enjoy activities.

8. Someone whose successes bring you pleasure.

9. Someone whose friendship you value so highly that you willingly make sacrifices to maintain it.

10. Someone whose absence for long periods of time produces loneliness.

By giving ten points to each of the above, you can quickly evaluate the quality of your friendship with a person, either your partner or someone else. As a general rule, you will probably enjoy a vital friendship with anyone who attracts a score of 80 points or more. But when you compare your feelings toward others with those toward your mate, keep in mind that if your relationship suffered as much exposure with someone else as it does with your mate, the score might drop drastically. Some people are great friends—if the relationship occurs only in small doses.

## The Essential Areas of Life

There are eight significant areas of life that produce accord and unity or else disharmony and conflict. Few couples start out with a 100 percent agreement on the priority they give to each area. Besides, as we have seen, people change through the years. Those who are very immature at 19 or 22 when they marry may begin to mature at 28 or 30.

If their mate does not progress to the same degree, they will someday be forced to acknowledge that few areas of common interest remain. Consequently they may become lonely, though living in the same home with a person they once enjoyed.

The key to longevity of friendship and marriage is mutual growth. Before I offer some suggestions on improving the degree of partner-friendship, it is important that you examine the most important areas of life.

## Agreement Is the Name of the Game

The Bible asks the crucial question, "How can two walk together except they are agreed?" The happiest relationships are those that enjoy the greatest amount of commonality. Study the eight essential areas of life carefully. Keep in mind that every individual attaches his own degree of importance to each of these areas. I list them in this order of importance from data gathered in the counseling room. These priorities may not always be completely accurate, of course, because people who come for help are troubled. Well-adjusted, happy couples seldom seek help, so their priorities might be different. Nevertheless, in one sense they are all important and should all be evaluated carefully.

## The Essential Areas of Life

### 1. Family

The area of life in which we spend the most time is family, and therefore it is probably the most important. That is confirmed in the landmark research of Dr. Robert Holmes, whose stress findings I have included in two of my other books. Suffice it to say here that the top seven stress-producing events revealed in his research all relate to the family. I conclude, therefore, that the most significant areas of life are those that produce the most stress when they malfunction.

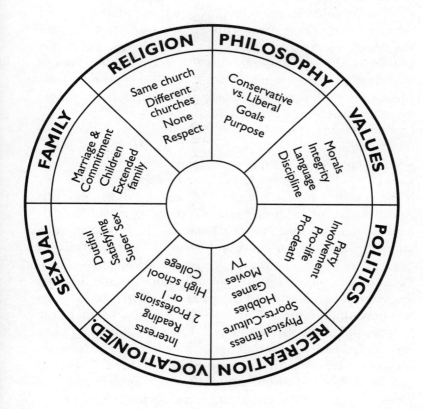

Diagram 14: Essentials of Life

The foundation of family is marriage and commitment—two people who intend to give of themselves exclusively to make their union meaningful and fulfilling for the other person. Then come children, the greatest treasure two people can share on this earth. They bring to the family indescribable joys and pleasures that cannot be experienced on any other human level. They also introduce pressures, trials, and sorrows, but even these can bind the family together with bonds that last a lifetime.

We should not overlook the extended family, which also has a binding effect on a couple's relationship. Ideally, when a couple marries, it is the marrying of two families. Good friends can be made of other members of the family if the couple has married with the blessing of the parents. Additionally, other family members often marry individuals with similar interests. My wife, for example, was 18 months younger than her sister and both went to Christian colleges because of their common interest in serving the Lord. Because my sister-in-law and her husband became missionaries and we both entered the pastorate, through the years we have maintained a strong friendship. In fact, my brother-in-law, whom I would never have known as a friend, has worked with me for half of our married lives because we married sisters. We are such close friends that I dedicated one of my books to him, and each year, together with our wives, we spend at least one week vacationing together.

Another part of the extended family concerns the grandchildren. What a joy! And no diaper-changing! Just cuddling (most of the time). The LaHaye annual water-skiing vacation at Lake Powell has grown through the years from 8 to 19 this year, and if the Lord tarries, the number will someday hit 25—a total of 25 people bound together by blood, marriage, interests, and friendship. Anything that involves one of those people is of vital concern to both members of the originating couple. (That is why after thinking my fatherly responsibilities to Little League and soccer were through, I find myself still attending games—and enjoying it.) Many other factors are included in "the family" area of life—furnishings, investments, etc. According to our Lord, "Where your treasure is, there will your heart be also." And if you haven't noticed, more of your time and money are spent on family than on anything else in life. Since time and money, humanly speaking, are their most important treasures, parents invest most of it in their children. The more I think about it, the more I believe I was right in selecting the family area first, because it is primary in importance.

## 2. Religious Persuasion

The Bible counsels, "Be not unequally yoked together with unbelievers." A person's faith, as we shall see, influences every other area of life.

That does not mean, however, that two believers will always share the same religious or church preference. For example, a Baptist can be attracted to an Episcopalian or either to a charismatic. These three churches share many core beliefs, but their forms of worship, teachings, and other beliefs are drastically different. Consequently, it is ideal when, in addition to a common personal faith, a couple meets at and attends the same church. Then it is easier to settle into a church of agreed choice and raise the family there. Because they are being taught the same doctrine, family members can develop deeper roots and friendships together.

I am not implying that couples who attend different churches cannot maintain a lasting love relationship. But it will, even under the best of conditions, put a strain on their relationship. That phenomenon is more pronounced when the differences are Protestant-Catholic or charismatic-noncharismatic. I regularly encourage couples to settle the church decision before the wedding. Usually the church which hosts the wedding is the place of worship which they plan to attend and someday raise their family.

The church is far more important to people today than ever before. Culturally it is the only consistent institutional friend upon which the family can depend. You will want a vital church with a strong emphasis on youth to provide a positive influence on your children, particularly when they become teenagers. Parents should never become divided over which church to attend as a family.

Visiting a variety of churches may be permissible before the children come along, but couples should by then agree on one church and raise their family in it. If you haven't found that kind of church yet, keep looking.

Unfortunately, many families today have no interest in church. When the storms of adversity begin to blow—and they will, for they are part of life—that family needs strong spiritual resources, which usually emanate from their church.

In some families only one person is interested in churchgoing. As a pastor, I knew many women who were married to "Sunday golfers." The marriage can still work if both partners are committed to each other and don't make Sunday activities a bone of contention, but even at best a lonely hole remains in a marriage, and the "split-Sunday syndrome" does nothing to help raise children in the faith, particularly when boys tend to follow their fathers. Some couples work out an "arrangement"; that is, they agree how frequently the active church member should attend church and how often the nonchurched should accompany him— particularly on special occasions, such as children's programs, Christmas, Easter, choir concerts, or special meetings. One of my friends agreed to attend "two services a month for the children's sake." He always complained, "That preacher is trying to convert me!" And he was right! But because he finally came, God changed his life and deeply enriched his marriage.

RESPECT is the key. You must respect your partner's religious beliefs even if you do not agree with them. Otherwise they will serve as a constant source of conflict and hinder the cementing of a friendship.

### 3. Philosophy of Life

It is all but impossible to exaggerate the importance of your philosophy of life. It influences almost every decision you make and everything you do. Your philosophy of life is what you are. From it flows your purpose for living, goals, and objectives. A workaholic bent on making millions of dollars reflects a materialistic philosophy of life that is limited to temporal values. One who keeps eternity's values in view "sets his affection on things above," maintaining an eternal philosophical perspective. Couples with such opposite philosophies will inevitably experience conflict.

Two words we are all familiar with today represent the dominant philosophy of life. One is "conservative," the other "liberal." Our entire nation is divided over the two philosophies described by those terms. "Liberals" believe in big government based on relativism and secular humanist ideas; government should supply all man's needs from the cradle to the grave. "Conservatives" believe in limited government and freedoms that mandate responsibility; every person is accountable to God and his fellowman for the way he lives his life. Conservatives usually espouse traditional values.

Liberals are not automatically communists or socialists, but they are not so different in their philosophy that they cannot concur readily with such groups. Conservatives, on the other hand, tend to be anti-communists who deplore the welfare state and espouse free enterprise and the free-market system. Liberals (though not all) tend to believe in a woman's "right to choose" an abortion if she needs one. Conservatives view abortion as murder. The list of almost diametric opposites is endless—pornography, situation ethics, the First Amendment, the right to bear arms, etc.

Doubtless a conservative and liberal husband and wife somewhere are enjoying a happy marriage, but I have never met such a pair. It would be difficult for them to hold a family discussion, for today almost everything would generate verbal conflict. They would subscribe to different magazines and reflect contrary opinions on all the issues of life. Every meal would be turned into a family "Crossfire" TV program. Unfortunately, it would not always be friendly; and many a night, because they fail to agree philosophically, they will go to bed loveless due to their disagreements.

Obviously, it is better when people with similar philosophical persuasions marry. If not, one should accept his partner's differing opinions and, for the sake of family harmony, rarely if ever discuss them. For example, can you envision two people happily married when one is a passivist and the other a supporter of the government's policy during a time of war? In such an arena of conflict, the couple could not even begin a discussion without raising room temperature to unlivable levels.

### 4. Values

A person's values are largely determined by his religious training, family customs, philosophy of life, and personal convictions. This has traditionally distinguished civilized people from barbarians. Those raised in Western culture have given value to virtue, morals, integrity, thrift, hard work, etc. A person's system of rights and wrongs determines his moral judgments. The closer a person is to Christian teachings, the more aligned he will be with "traditional values" or Christian values.

Values have become blurred today by the rise of relativism, producing what Charles Colson calls "New Barbarians,"

Westerners with a high degree of education and a liberal-secular humanist view of morals. To them, nothing is absolute; rights and wrongs are indeterminate, and in the moral realm "nothing is a big deal."

It doesn't take much imagination to determine that anyone with traditional values will have a difficult time loving, respecting, and enjoying a close friendship with someone who does not share that value system but instead is willing to lie, cheat, steal, and break his commitment to wedding vows. Usually disharmony becomes so strong that such people do not get together in the first place. However, if one partner submits his will to Christ, his values will change, opening the door to conflict.

In such situations, the Christian must trust God for the grace to live happily with his unsaved mate and give him patience not to criticize or look disrespectfully on the partner because of these differences. Otherwise he will destroy their friendship. Two cannot walk together very long unless they are agreed on moral values.

### 5. Politics

You have doubtless heard the old expression "There are two things you never discuss unless you want to get into an argument—religion and politics." I would agree with that assessment. However, if we don't discuss those subjects, we eliminate about 60 percent of what is worth talking about in life. And today, with CNN and network news booming into our homes every night, almost the entire country is turning into "news junkies." Most of the controversial issues of our day—from the importance of life in the first trimester of pregnancy to the United States playing world cop at the risk of bankrupting future generations—is introduced directly into the home. And when couples disagree politically, they may sink from lively dissent to abrasive argumentation.

It is best, of course, if both partners share a common interest in the same political parties, particularly if either or both become active on behalf of some candidate. The alternative is to keep their opinions to themselves and respect the partner's right to hold a contrary view. Two partners I know belong to opposing political parties. Driving home on election night, the husband listened to the election news as his candidate was plummeting to defeat in ignominious flames. Walking past his wife, who was awaiting his affectionate greeting, he announced, "I'm not ready to kiss a Republican yet!" Fortunately for them, they enjoy many other areas of agreement, so political preference does not destroy their friendship.

### 6. Recreation and Entertainment

"Jack" became a very "dull boy" because to him life was "all work and no play." The couple that doesn't learn to play together won't stay together, at least very happily. In a dating situation couples seem to have little trouble finding things to enjoy doing together. They may not realize, of course, that it is the *time* they share that knits them together, and not the activity itself. After marriage, when they are together all the time, they may begin to admit that they don't really like the same activities.

A wise partner will learn what brings enjoyment to his spouse. We are a water-skiing, snow-skiing, camping, and dirt-motorcycle-riding family. Not everything brings equal pleasure, but an unselfish person will learn to do what his partner finds enjoyable. That is the motivation of love. Common pleasures tend to broaden areas of common interest, and this is true with games, entertainment, and other activities. Try to cultivate the same sporting interests; share the rules, the significance of certain games, and any stories about the players. Naturally, all things must be done with moderation, but it is vitally important that couples and families learn to play together.

### 7. Education and Vocation

For centuries only husbands received more than a standard education; consequently there was often a great disparity in the intellectual development of couples. Today it is not uncommon for both partners to have an equal education, and in almost 70 percent of the cases both husband and wife work vocationally outside the home, usually in different companies and in different trades. Consequently, unless they make a conscious effort to acquaint themselves with their partner's vocation by long conversations and interested questioning, during large blocks of time they will share no common vocational interests. This is not all bad if both partners can learn to leave the vocational world at work and enjoy family environment when they are home.

Magazines can become a useful supplement to one's education and can stimulate common interests. Every home, if financially able, should subscribe to magazines, both Christian and secular, that will contribute to a common philosophy. In fact, one can almost identify the philosophy of a person by his favorite magazines. A liberal Christian friend with whom I argue every time we meet reads *Time, Newsweek,* and *U.S. News.* I canceled those subscriptions years ago because of their liberal stance, replacing them with *Human Events, Insight,* and *National Review.* Can you imagine how my friend and I would argue if he read *The Village Voice* or Moscow's favorite, *Mother Jones?*

Many Christian families strengthen their mental and emotional fabric daily with Christian radio. Others feed their souls with wholesome cassettes and videos. Be sure of this: The education you receive, whether formal or through voluntary reading and listening, carries a philosophy and will directly influence your thinking patterns and perspectives. It is important that couples show an interest in each other's education and reading.

### 8. Sex Life

Even though I have already mentioned the importance of a good sex life in marriage, I would be remiss in not once again calling to your attention that it is a vital arena that helps partners to become best friends. Depending on their understanding of the experience and their mastery of the art of self-control, couples can experience anything from super sex to dutiful activity. Never take intimacy for granted; try to keep it fresh and alive, and always an expression of love. For many couples whose areas of common interest is deficient, they are able to rectify it through "super sex," or even very satisfying sex. Any relationship will be enhanced by a dynamic love life.

## The Missing Ingredient

You have probably noticed the hole in the middle of my circular chart (Diagram 14, page 267), which was left blank by design. Two important centers will affect every area of your life. As seen on the next page, one is marked FAITH and the other UNBELIEF.

These two circles are designed to drop into the circle of life interests. If a person has a vital personal faith in God, it will influence every area of his life. I once asked a custom home contractor what change he noted in his life after he accepted Christ as Lord and Savior. He responded, "My values changed. Before Christ, when a customer called to ask a question, I would rack my brain to remember what I told him the last time. Now I just tell the truth; I know that will be the same message that I gave him before." Jesus Christ changes people, mostly in the very areas discussed on the circle.

# *Two-Circle Chart*

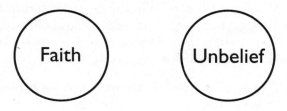

By contrast, the unbeliever undergoes little change—at least not in the direction of biblical principles. That is why it is so important for married partners to agree on their personal relationship to Jesus Christ. So again I would stress that if you do not have a vital relationship with God, you need to invite His Son into your heart and receive His Holy Spirit. It is a life-changing experience that will enrich every area of your life. And no one can help two people become best friends better than Christ. Do you know Him? Does your partner know Him? If not, receive Him personally by inviting Him into your heart today. If you don't know how to pray but believe that Jesus Christ died for your sins, was buried, and rose from the dead, please utter this prayer or one like it in your heart: "O God, I am a sinner. I do believe that Jesus died on the cross for my sins. This day I invite Him to come into my life, forgive my sins, and save my soul. I give what is left of my life to You."

Such a prayer has saved the lives of millions of people and introduced a whole new dimension to their lives. Jesus said, "I am come that you might have life and that you might have it more abundantly." He wants to have an abundant impact on every area of your life. And you are the only one who can let Him.

## Summary

Friendship-marriage is not just an impossible ideal; with God's help it is possible, even in the face of vast differences, whether they be temperament, education, beliefs, or preferences. But it will take conscious effort. Here in summary are some final suggestions:

1. Share a lifetime commitment to each other and your family.

2. As much as possible, try to develop a common philosophy of life.

3. Attempt to cultivate a sincere interest in your partner's likes, work, and interests.

4. Learn to enjoy the accomplishments of your partner as well as those things that give your partner pleasure.

5. Be honest, up-front, and loyal to your partner.

6. Unselfishly work to help your partner become successful and accomplish his or her dreams and destiny.

7. Try to remove from your life those things that irritate your partner.

8. Always show respect for your partner's beliefs and decisions even when you disagree with them.

Good friendships are among life's most valuable assets, worthy of any reasonable sacrifice. Most unfriendly partners live lonely lives without the central quality of meaningful human experience—true companionship. Usually that can be corrected. Stripped of the accepted facade of causes, loneliness in marriage means that one or both partners were too selfish to make whatever sacrifices were necessary to become best friends.

Friendship is its own reward.

## Best Friends Even in Death

Frank and Carrie were married over 60 years. I was their pastor for 15 of those years, and Frank was the kind of godly deacon that should happen to every pastor. It was easy to see that they loved each other. Better than that, they were each other's best friend. And while God never gave them children, they lived a rich, full life of companionship. When Frank took sick, Carrie nursed him for nine months before he died. Three days later Carrie, who had not been ill, slumped over at the breakfast table dead. Doctors could find no cause for her death—except loneliness.

When the undertaker called me I said, "Let's delay Frank's funeral for two days and conduct them together in the church." I announced the memorial service on Sunday and, needless to say, the church was packed. We did not hold a wake for Frank and Carrie—just a praise service. We thanked God for saving them, for their long and faithful lives, and for the friendship that gave meaning to life for as long as they both lived. Now they are enjoying the ultimate in companionship, together with our Lord, where they will never again be separated.

If the Lord tarries and if we live that long, that is how Bev and I would like to go—together.

# The Christian Couple's Secret Weapon

A frantic call came from a distraught mother in Tucson, Arizona. "My son Rick and his wife Jan live there in San Diego and are going to file for divorce on Thursday, but they promised to see a minister if I found one who would counsel them. My pastor knows you and has read all your books. He said you would meet with them."

To be very honest, my counseling load at the time was about to drown me; I didn't need any out-of-state additions. But before I could say no, this deeply burdened mother added the magic words, "They have three children!" No Christian counselor I know could turn down an opportunity like that.

When they arrived on Tuesday night, they were obviously just fulfilling an obligation to Rick's mother before destroying a marriage of 13 years. Rick started by saying, "Pastor, forgive us for wasting your time. There is nothing that can save this marriage." To prove his point he continued, "We have been to a Christian counseling center in Los Angeles. The counselor gave us a battery of psychological tests and found that we were so hopelessly mismatched that we ought to get a divorce!" Suddenly my body juices began pumping, for whoever came to that conclusion did not understand the power of God. Then Rick gave me the best lead-in I've ever had: "What do you think of that advice?"

I replied, "What *I* think about it is really not important (I didn't want to tell them it was the worst advice I had ever heard). But you do need to hear what God says about it." Turning to 1 Corinthians 7:10,27, I read these words: "Now to the married I command, yet not I but the Lord: A wife is not to depart from her husband. . . . Are you bound to a wife? Do not seek to be loose." I shall never forget Rick's response. With a typical Chlor-San sneer on his face he challenged, "You mean God wants us to be this miserable the rest of our lives?"

"No," I explained, "God wants you to be happy the rest of your lives, but it will never come by disobeying His precepts." I then introduced them to the principles in this book, all of which are based on the Word of God, which was intended, among other things, to show people how to be happy, particularly married couples. "Since God is the author of marriage," I continued, "He intended it to be the most sublime relationship two people can share on this earth." They could not experience the joy of marriage, even though they were Christians, because they were selfishly disobeying several of God's basic principles.

Fortunately for their children, one on the mission field today and the other two in established Christian homes, those two parents got down on their knees with me and re-surrendered their wills to God. They admitted their sins— he of selfish anger, she of selfish fears—and today they enjoy a model relationship.

While we were on our knees I suddenly realized that we had come to a position of new beginnings, and I have used this approach many times since. Almost all couples enter into marriage on their knees before God. Remember your wedding? As soon as the minister pronounced you man and wife, he led you to kneel at the prayer bench or the altar as an act of humble submission, followed by a prayer that invoked God's blessings on your brand-new home and relationship. But very honestly, happiness in marriage is based not on the minister's prayer but on your continued acts of compliance with the will of God.

Unfortunately for most couples, that symbolic act of prayer is nothing more than a meaningless ritual. But couples who pray regularly together rarely experience a need for marriage counseling. Discord arises for two reasons: Partners fail to pray together, and they are not really surrendered to the will and guidance of God.

Several times Scripture promises, "Happy is he who hears the Word of God and keeps it." Our Lord's statement makes it clear that the road to happiness lies not in seeking our own way but in fulfilling His desires.

God's way is always best, even when it seems anything but right, fair, or attractive. The couple that proceeds to follow the will of God by faith is the couple that delights in a happy marriage.

## Life's Crisis Point

Every person and almost every marriage will face a crisis point when one or both people think they cannot endure the conflict, disagreement, and pressure one moment longer. But instead of flying into a rage and aggravating each other, they must learn to surrender the problem, their life, and their will to God. He has a plan for us whether we know it or not. As an act of faith, we must submit ourselves at that moment to the fulfillment of His will.

The apostle Paul on the road to Damascus is a classic example. He met his crisis point with full surrender by turning to Christ with the prayer, "Lord, what will You have me to do?" Thousands of people have prayed similar prayers at crisis points, from Augustine, John Wesley, D.L. Moody, and Billy Graham to you and me.

When couples humbly surrender their wills to God in prayer during times of crisis, they have taken the first step toward resolving their differences and conflicts.

## How to Handle Differences

My wife and I are both strong-willed people. Any woman who can appear before the U.S. Senate Judiciary Committee to be interrogated by the likes of Senators Ted Kennedy, Joe Biden, Howard Metzenbaum, and other liberals who are openly hostile to advocates of traditional values, yet comes away without losing her composure, has to be strong-willed (or, more accurately, the recipient of divine power through prayer). During his last term of office, President Bush asked Bev to testify at the confirmation hearings for Judges Scalia, Bork, and Kennedy. And she doesn't suppress that strong will and determined drive when she comes home at night.

I am not exactly a pushover myself—after all, during my 33 years as a pastor I attended at least 330 deacon meetings, 315 trustee sessions, and at least 10,000 other "bored" meetings, either serving as moderator or sitting in the hot seat. As your pastor and most pastoral search committees will tell you, "only the strong need apply." Both Bev and I are opinionated, determined, or strong-willed people. If I said we agreed on everything, I would be lying. It would be closer to the truth to admit that we disagree on almost everything—except those issues for which we have already established guidelines.

As I noted earlier, if there are two ways to do something or go somewhere, she will choose one and I the other. Yet today we enjoy a fabulous relationship. Why? Because differences never cause us to lose respect for each other. We even respectfully recognize the right of our partner to be wrong. We have also learned to pray about our differences. When Bev prefers one pathway and I have made a different choice, we have learned to commit our difference to God.

Such a prayer time isn't particularly structured—just honest. We get down on our knees and admit to God that our preferences are at cross-purposes. Then we commit the decision to Him, assured that He has a will for our lives. Since we know by faith that His plan is best, we submit our wills to Him in advance and pray the model prayer of our Savior, "Nevertheless, not my will but Yours be done." Without exception, God has responded in one of two ways: He has either caused one of us to change our mind and fully accept the other person's plan or desire, or else he has opened our eyes to a totally different plan. We have bought houses, identified a discipline technique for our children, mapped out vacations, accepted speaking engagements, and even agreed on the number of children via such prayers.

As we look back, we never second-guess those prayerfully made decisions or plans. The ones we regret—or at least would make differently if we had the decisions to make over—are those we neglected to pray about. We try to take literally the scriptural admonition, "In all your ways acknowledge *Him* and He will direct your path."

## Regular Couple Prayer

After conducting over 700 Family Life Seminars for close to a million people during these last 26 years, I receive one comment consistently: "The principle we learned from your seminar that helped our marriage most was your instruction on 'couple prayer.'" Since this book concerns the resolution of differences and conflicts in marriage, I would like to capsulize that thought for you here at the close. If you are not using it now, I guarantee that it will improve your relationship.

At the outset I am not talking about or excluding private devotions or times of worship with the entire family. I heartily recommend both. I am talking about a conversational method of prayer that is simple and extremely meaningful. It reduces differences of temperament, background, taste, and will to a manageable level, preventing injurious clashes.

Couple prayer is a form of conversational prayer with your partner. The ground rules are very simple. On the first night the husband should lead, praying for the initial burden on his heart for 30 seconds to two minutes, after which he stops, but without concluding, "In Jesus' name, Amen," for that would signal an end to the prayer. His pause allows his wife to provide an addendum, praying briefly for that same burden. When she finishes, she too just stops. At that point the husband introduces the second burden on his heart, after which the wife responds in kind. Each time she will address the issue from her perspective, addressing God in ways that did not occur to him.

As a rule we seldom pray about more than five burdens during each session, for with a second participation that means ten short prayers, extending the session to 20 or 30 minutes. We did eight burdens one night and found that 16 participations lasted almost an hour. As a rule only heavily burdened couples will have that much time for prayer.

The second night it is the wife's turn to lead with her first burden, the husband following each petition with his heart's concerns. Whoever starts the evening prayer should give the signal to conclude by injecting "in Jesus' name we pray, Amen."

Such prayer has an incredible way of binding two people together. It will not only enrich their love but bond them mentally and spiritually. Within two weeks one of the partners will inevitably lead in prayer for a burden that started on his partner's heart. Obviously they now have joint heart burdens, which creates a powerful bonding! We have discovered that we often share concerns during prayer times that we forget to discuss on the conscious level. Later one of us will turn to the other and ask, "What happened with so and so?" and the person listening will respond, "When did we discuss that?" Actually, we didn't—except in couple prayer. We have also experienced the sessions of joy and gratitude when we get to thank God for His solution or His answer to one or more of those prayers. I know nothing that will grind off differences between partners or bind two people together better than couple prayer. Just make sure each expression is addressed to *God,* not to each other. Perpendicular prayers are good; horizontal prayers may damage a relationship.

Remember the couple that came to my office on Tuesday night before seeing the attorney? They were the first couple I introduced to this kind of couple prayer, 30 years ago. They haven't changed temperaments, but they certainly have learned to respect, love, and cherish each other. Couple prayer for them was a lifesaver, not only enriching their relationship but rescuing their marriage.

Try it. It will enhance your capacity to love and become best friends—even if you are total opposites.

# How to Have Your
# Temperament Diagnosed

*A Personal Letter from Dr. LaHaye*

Dear Reader:

During the past 25 years I have worked diligently to develop a test that would accurately diagnose a person's temperament and then show him how to strengthen his weaknesses so he could utilize all the talents and creativity that God has provided him at conception. After designing four separate tests and administering them to hundreds of people, I finally devised the "LaHaye Temperament Analysis."

To date, my staff and I have given this test to and written analyses more than 33,000 people. From the correspondence I have received, it must be very accurate, for many are profuse in their expressions of appreciation.

Many people consider the personalized analysis I prepare after they have taken the test to be the most helpful response of its kind. This analysis will—

- identify your primary and secondary temperament and many of your traits.

- provide 50 vocational fields that you would be suited for.

- suggest three work habits you may need to work on.

- list your spiritual gifts in their priority and provide 25 areas in your church where you could most profitably serve.

- identify your ten greatest weaknesses and show you how to overcome them through spiritual resources.

- identify the most significant mistakes your temperament usually makes in interpersonal relationships and provide other suggestions as to improvement of your marriage and family life.

- if you're single, offer suggestions on how to present yourself more effectively to the opposite sex.

- warn those with children of pitfalls to avoid in childraising.

# The Cost

Similar tests cost from $50 to $200, according to many people who have attended my seminars. But these same people considered the LaHaye Temperament Analysis far more helpful and practical, and I am confident that you will too, at the current price of only $29.95, less the enclosed $10 discount coupon.

# Instructions

Mail the enclosed coupon with $19.95 for each test ordered. The coupon, which can be used for two $10 discounts (married or engaged couples), must accompany the order and payment. Upon receipt of your check, we will send your test booklet and return envelope immediately. When your test arrives, it should be filled out at one sitting (30–40 minutes).

As soon as it is returned to our office, we will process it, analyze it, and write you a personalized analysis or report. I am confident you will be glad you did.

Sincerely yours,

*Tim LaHaye*

· · · · · · · · · · · · · **Discount Coupon** · · · · · · · · · · · · · · ·

- Discover your personality type for only $19.95 (that's $10 off the regular price) and enjoy the benefits of knowing yourself better.

- To receive your personalized temperament analysis, write your name and address on this discount certificate and send it with your check (please, U.S. funds only) for $19.95 to:

**Family Life Ministries**
P.O. Box 2700
Washington, DC 20013-2700

Name _____

Address _____

City _____ State _____ Zip _____

# *Notes*

**Chapter 10—Other Differences**

1. Dr. James C. Dobson, *Straight Talk to Men and Their Wives*, pp. 161-62.
2. Ibid., p. 163.
3. Daniel Goleman, "Subtle but Intriguing Differences Found in the Brain Anatomy of Men and Women," *The New York Times*, April 11, 1989, C1.
4. Ibid., p. C6.
5. Daniel Goleman, "Study Defines Major Sources of Conflict Between Sexes," *The New York Times*, June 13, 1989, p. C14.
6. Malcolm Gladwell, "Women and Depression: Culture Called a Key Factor," *The Washington Post*, December 6, 1990, p. A1.

**Chapter 11—Giant Step One**

7. David Field, *Marriage Personalities* (Eugene, OR: Harvest House) 1986, p. 128.
8. Ibid.
9. Ibid., p. 131.
10. Ibid.

# About the Author

Tim LaHaye is a noted author, minister, counselor, television commentator, and nationally recognized speaker on family life and Bible prophecy. He is the founder and president of Family Life Seminars and founder of The PreTrib Research Center. He is also the father of four children and grandfather of nine. Snow skiing, water skiing, motorcycling, golfing, family vacations, and jogging are among his leisure activities.

LaHaye is a graduate of Bob Jones University, and holds an M.A. and Doctor of Ministry degree from Western Conservative Theological Seminary.

For 25 years he pastored one of the nation's outstanding churches in San Diego, California which grew to three locations. During that time he also founded two accredited Christian high schools, a Christian school system of ten schools, Christian Heritage College, and other ministry-related organizations.

LaHaye has written 39 books on a wide range of subjects, including: family life, temperaments, sexual adjustment, Bible prophecy, the will of God, Jesus Christ, and secular humanism. His current fiction series written with Jerry Jenkins, *Left Behind, Tribulation Force,* and *Nicolae,* which are leading hundreds to Christ, are the number-one fiction bestsellers among Christian books. These prophetic novels are based on Bible prophecy as portrayed by fictitious characters who live through the tribulation as new believers in Christ.

There are over 10 million copies of LaHaye books in print, some of which have been translated into 32 foreign languages. His writings are best noted for their easy-to-understand and scripturally based applications of biblical principles that assist in facing and handling the challenges of life.

# Other Good
# Harvest House Reading

## HOW TO STUDY THE BIBLE FOR YOURSELF
by *Tim LaHaye*

This excellent book provides fascinating study helps and charts that will make personal Bible study more interesting and exciting. A three-year program is outlined to help you gain a better working knowledge of the Bible.

## THE POWER OF A PRAYING WIFE
by *Stormie Omartian*

Every wife who desires a deeper, more meaningful relationship with her husband will appreciate Stormie Omartian's candor and encouragement in this insightful, practical book. Stormie teaches women how to pray for their husbands in more than 30 areas, including decision-making, faith, fears, spiritual strength, sexuality, and communication.

## QUIET TIMES FOR COUPLES
by *H. Norman Wright*

This bestselling collection of 365 warm, personal devotions was gleaned from Wright's many years of helping couples experience togetherness in Christ.

## THE SPIRIT-CONTROLLED WOMAN
by *Beverly LaHaye*

This bestseller gives the Christian woman practical help in understanding herself and the weaknesses she encounters in her private life and in her relationships. Every stage of a woman's life is included, with practical, Biblical counsel.

### UNDERSTANDING THE LAST DAYS
by *Tim LaHaye*

If you ever wanted to come to your own understanding of Bible prophecy and current events but were unsure where to begin, *Understanding the Last Days* was written especially for you. In this straightforward, easy-to-understand guide, you'll discover the tools and knowledge you need to help you accurately interpret biblical prophecy.

### UNDERSTANDING YOUR CHILD'S TEMPERAMENT
by *Beverly LaHaye*

Family advocate Beverly LaHaye shows parents how an understanding of their child's personality type can help them teach, discipline, relate to, and encourage their children. The basic temperaments and their blends are addressed to help you appreciate your child's uniqueness.

### WHAT MAKES A MAN FEEL LOVED
by *Bob Barnes*

Although men and women were made for each other, it sometimes seems like men are from a completely different planet! *What Makes a Man Feel Loved* gives you an opportunity to step into your husband's world. Written by a man, this unusual book reveals what you can do to enhance the excitement and vibrancy of your marriage.

*Harvest House Books by*
*Tim & Beverly LaHaye*

How to Study the Bible for Yourself
How to Study Bible Prophecy for Yourself
Opposites Attract
The Spirit-Filled Family
The Spirit-Controlled Woman
Understanding Your Child's Temperament

Dear Reader,

We would appreciate hearing from you regarding this Harvest House non-fiction book. It will enable us to continue to give you the best in Christian publishing.

1. What most influenced you to purchase *Opposites Attract?*
   - ❑ Author
   - ❑ Subject matter
   - ❑ Backcover copy
   - ❑ Recommendations
   - ❑ Cover/Title
   - ❑ Other_____

2. Where did you purchase this book?
   - ❑ Christian bookstore
   - ❑ General bookstore
   - ❑ Department store
   - ❑ Grocery store
   - ❑ Other_____

3. Your overall rating of this book?
   - ❑ Excellent  ❑ Very good  ❑ Good  ❑ Fair  ❑ Poor

4. How likely would you be to purchase other books by this author?
   - ❑ Very likely  ❑ Not very likely  ❑ Somewhat likely  ❑ Not at all

5. What types of books most interest you? (Check all that apply.)
   - ❑ Women's Books
   - ❑ Marriage Books
   - ❑ Current Issues
   - ❑ Self Help/Psychology
   - ❑ Bible Studies
   - ❑ Fiction
   - ❑ Biographies
   - ❑ Children's Books
   - ❑ Youth Books
   - ❑ Other_____

6. Please check the box next to your age group.
   - ❑ Under 18  ❑ 18-24  ❑ 25-34  ❑ 35-44  ❑ 45-54  ❑ 55 and over

**Mail to:**  Editorial Director
Harvest House Publishers
1075 Arrowsmith
Eugene, OR 97402

Name_____

Address_____

State _____ Zip _____

**Thank you for helping us to help you in future publications!**